AF348608

THE ECONOMICS OF FREEDOM

THE ECONOMICS OF FREEDOM

IN DEFENSE OF CAPITALISM

DAVID F. RANKIN
with **BETH ANNE RANKIN**

Archway Publishing books may be ordered through booksellers or by contacting:

Archway Publishing
1663 Liberty Drive
Bloomington, IN 47403
www.archwaypublishing.com
844-669-3957

ISBN: 978-1-6657-4768-4 (sc)
ISBN: 978-1-6657-4770-7 (hc)
ISBN: 978-1-6657-4769-1 (e)

Library of Congress Control Number: 2023914207

Print information available on the last page.

Archway Publishing rev. date: 10/31/2023

CONTENTS

Early in my years as a college professor of economics and finance, I came under the influence of four brilliant economics professors who dramatically affected my professional life. I later had an opportunity to meet and visit with all four and discuss many of the topics I had only read about in their publications.

The first was Milton Friedman, who won the 1979 Nobel Prize in economics. After hearing him speak at Harding University here in Arkansas, I quickly read his blockbuster book *Free to Choose.* That was it; I was hooked! The powerful logic and insight of this man were incredible. He presented economic ideas with tremendous clarity. Friedman was far ahead of his time; many of his ideas continue to be discussed and implemented today.

The second was Walter Williams, at the time an economics professor at George Mason University. As the Murphy Lecturer at my university in the 1980s, Williams wholly impressed me with his teaching ability. He took to the stage with only a chalkboard, and yet he kept the audience spellbound with vivid examples and memorable stories. His presentation on the downside of the minimum wage provided a powerful example regarding the difference between economic *intentions* and economic *results.*

The third was Thomas Sowell, senior fellow at the Hoover Institute, who spoke at Southern Arkansas University in the 1990s. Professor Sowell continues to send me copies of his books, and they belong on everyone's must-read list. His 2018 book, *Discrimination and Disparities,* is outstanding and a great example of the brilliant mind of this man.

The fourth was Arthur Laffer, who came to my university for a lecture in 1981. He had become famous for his Laffer Curve, which became the basis for tax cuts under the Reagan administration. The basic premise of the curve is that income tax rates can become so high that total tax revenue actually decreases when rates are raised. He argued that, at this point, tax cuts can actually increase total tax revenue rather than reduce it.

These four economics professors impacted not only me personally but the entire national debate regarding the economics of liberty. They each carried the torch for economic freedom, and their scholarship will continue to powerfully influence future generations of Americans.

INTRODUCTION

At this point in history, the United States of America reigns as the most powerful economic and military nation on the planet. It is a lofty perch, and the competition is on the hunt to dethrone our nation from its preeminent position. Unfortunately, powerful and influential forces exist even within our own borders that seem intent on instituting national policies that would reduce our ability to maintain our world leadership position.

I often remind my students to "compare the real with the real." Critics of the United States can undoubtedly find fault; we do, after all, exist in the human condition. However, to draw real conclusions, we need to compare our nation with other real nations in the real world. We can then draw practical, valuable, and realistic conclusions.

The United States has been successful for a number of reasons. Primary among these is that except for the Civil War (1861-1865), the US has had a robust run of internal peace and order. The rule of law has been the order of the day. At the peak of the Roman Empire's power (Pax Romana), similar conditions prevailed.

Many countries across the globe have not been so fortunate. War, civil unrest, and corruption are powerful enemies of economic development. Nations continually beset by turmoil trail those nations that avoid such difficulties.

The US has also been blessed with abundant natural resources and an agreeable climate. However, many other nations can claim the same. The essential ingredient, in my opinion, has been the existence of an incredible level of freedom enjoyed by our citizens. Freedom liberates the creative talents of citizens and empowers them to pursue work, innovation, and enterprise with few restrictions.

Lord Denning, a leading figure in British justice during the 1900s, penned this statement about freedom:

> Each man should be free to develop his own personality to the full; the only duties which should restrict this freedom should be those which are necessary to enable everyone else to do the same.[1]

Most modern governments have departed from this freedom-embracing principle. Regrettably, almost every developed nation's government has a tendency to issue reams of rules, regulations, and tax requirements limiting individual freedom in a wide variety of ways.

President Thomas Jefferson, in his first inaugural address on March 4, 1801, described the newly formed government of the United States as the "world's best hope" and articulated the ideal role of government:

> A wise and frugal government, which shall restrain men from injuring one another, shall leave them otherwise free to regulate their own pursuits of industry and improvement, and shall not take from the mouth of labor the bread it has earned.[2]

American colonists in the 1770s had their fill of the intrusive and oppressive British government of the time. The result? The American Revolution and a bold claim for freedom by the new American citizens. King George III was replaced with an elected president and Congress.

Government is necessary to preserve a free society, but it must be limited. Today, far too many citizens are ready to exchange precious freedom for promised benefits that may or may not ever appear. We need to protect the power, pleasure, and benefits of freedom. We need to fully understand the role of economics policy with regard to freedom. More pointedly, we need to understand *The Economics of Freedom.*

CHAPTER 1

FREEDOM: THE ESSENTIAL ELEMENT

THE CONCEPT OF FREEDOM MEANS MANY DIFFERENT THINGS TO different people. To some it might mean a responsibility-free weekend. To others it could mean the beginning of summer vacation, the payoff of a burdensome mortgage, or the completion of a two-week stay in the county jail. However, to many, it has a much deeper and more emotional meaning.

The New Oxford American Dictionary defines freedom as a noun meaning "the power or right to act, speak, or think as one wants without hindrance or restraint." Notice this definition puts the emphasis on acting, speaking, and thinking. The US Declaration of Independence emphasizes similar sentiments.

> We hold these truths to be self-evident, that all men are created equal, that they are endowed by their creator with certain unalienable Rights, that among these are Life, Liberty, and the pursuit of Happiness.[1]

Authored by Thomas Jefferson, the Declaration was edited by the Committee of Five: John Adams, Benjamin Franklin, Roger Sherman, Thomas Jefferson, and Robert Livingston. It was further edited by the Committee of the Whole of the Second Continental Congress and adopted on July 4, 1776.[2]

Thus, the American experiment began in a landscape of almost total freedom of enterprise. The central government was quite small in those days and did not have the ability to interfere much with daily life. The new citizens of the fledgling United States could do pretty much what they wanted, if they did not harm their fellow citizens. Shamefully, this promise of life and liberty was not extended to all until much later in our nation's history. The ideal was there, but the application was not. It took the brutal Civil War and years of struggle for all Americans to be free to enjoy the ideals of the Declaration of Independence and the Constitution. Anytime an individual or group of individuals has limited opportunity or none, the whole nation suffers a reduction in social cohesiveness, economic growth, and prosperity.

It is clear that the nation's founders viewed government as an institution designed to promote life and liberty, not to interfere with it. This is in striking contrast to the view that citizens exist to support and provide government with the resources to do what it wants to do. All too often we hear the refrain from government leaders that they need more money. It is important to remember that governments *always* tend to say they need more money.

> There is no art which one government sooner learns
> of another than that of draining money from the
> pockets of the people.[3] (Adam Smith)

The signers of the Declaration of Independence were well aware of the abuses of government. As British colonists, they were continually reminded of the intrusive power of the British authorities. It is fascinating that Jefferson, in the Declaration of Independence, observed that King George III "has erected a multitude of new offices and sent hither swarms of officers to harass our people, and eat out their substance."[4]

Governments of all sorts seem eager to engage in these activities as they grow larger. If you hire one thousand government employees and send them to Washington, DC, to regulate something, that is exactly what they will do. This will go on forty hours each week, fifty-two weeks each year, year after year, decade after decade, and ofttimes much longer. It is just the nature of the beast. Many of these government activities continue long after they are needed.

According to scholars R. J. Teare and H. L. McPheeters: "In 1803, the British created a civil service job calling for a man to stand on the Cliffs of Dover with a spy glass. He was supposed to ring a bell if he saw Napoleon coming. The job was abolished in 1945."[5] Napoleon had been dead for 124 years.

Having seen government heavy-handedness, interference, and inefficiency firsthand, the founders resolved to avoid a repeat. This is why the Declaration of Independence and the Constitution are so specific about individual freedom. The Bill of Rights (the first ten amendments to the Constitution) ratified on December 15, 1791, guaranteed very particular rights to all American citizens. The Bill of Rights protects individual freedom. Author William F. Buckley Jr. described the Bill of Rights as a "Ten Commandments, a syllabus of constraints."[6] It is essential to note the entity that needs to be constrained is government, not individuals. By careful design, the Bill of Rights enumerates distinct and specific freedoms, liberties, and rights of the *people.*

If you take a careful look at each amendment, you will recognize numerous amendments we are failing to administer appropriately today. For example, how about a fair and speedy trial? How about the liberty to speak freely? How about the ability to express personal religious beliefs without interference?

There are those who would lead us away from freedom in their quest for influence and power. The founders designed the Bill of Rights to prevent such activities. It is vital that we, as American citizens, become very familiar with each of these amendments. Our future depends on it.

AMENDMENT I

> Congress shall make no law respecting an establishment of religion, or prohibiting the free exercise thereof; or abridging the freedom of speech, or of the press, or the right of the people peaceably to assemble, and to petition the Government for a redress of grievances.

Looking at the First Amendment in today's context, it is easy to see that the right of citizens to express their views is under attack. In the last several years, individuals have been fired from their jobs, canceled from social media, and subjected to harassment because of their political opinions, religious beliefs, and other politically incorrect positions. A political firestorm erupted when the National School Boards Association sent a letter to the Department of Justice comparing concerned parents who showed up at school board meetings across the country to *domestic terrorists*.[7] Many feared the DOJ would actually move forward with labeling these parents domestic terrorists. What was the parents' crime? They expressed concern about issues ranging from COVID-19-related mask mandates to some of the things their children were being taught in the controversial area of race theory. Fortunately, any potential DOJ labeling initiative was throttled after an uproar. However, there is no question we have entered a new era of social discourse where free expression is often attacked.

The rise of the woke culture in recent years threatens freedom of speech and expression. If freedom of speech really exists, some people are going to be offended and may take exception to something said or presented. That comes with the freedom territory. With freedom of speech comes the freedom to be offended. If you are offended, say so. But to attack fellow citizens' livelihoods and reputations just because you are offended is ridiculous. State your case. Offer your logic. Debate the issue. If citizens do not feel free to express their opinions on issues, how free are they? Just because someone disagrees with me does not mean they are evil. We must be able to disagree and still be civil.

> To silence criticism is to silence freedom.[8] (Sidney Hook, American philosopher)

Citizens in many nations throughout the world are afraid to express themselves. On a trip to the USSR in 1991 just before its collapse, a Soviet citizen told me that when her daughter was growing up, she allowed her to read the epic novel *Doctor Zhivago* on the sly. She warned her daughter to be sure and not mention at school that she was reading the book, as it was banned by Soviet authorities. She feared the consequences. This is not something we want to happen in the United States. Freedom of speech is essential to freedom. This is precisely why free speech has such a prominent position in the Constitution. In the First Amendment, it is listed second, right after freedom of religion.

The interference of some state authorities with the right to assemble to worship during the pandemic of 2020 is another example of trampling on the First Amendment. Also, during the pandemic, authorities often picked winners and losers by determining who was allowed to continue to operate and who was not. Many of these decisions had little rhyme or reason.

The First Amendment is first for a reason. The freedom of religion, freedom of speech, freedom of the press, the right to assemble peacefully, and the right to petition to address grievances are all cornerstones of freedom itself. A little study of history will remind all of us that governments frequently want to limit these freedoms in their quest for power and uniformity. It is important to note the amendment starts out with the phrase "Congress shall make no law ….” The erosion of freedom within a free society starts with attacks on free speech and, in our case, the First Amendment.

AMENDMENT II

> A well-regulated Militia, being necessary to the security of a free State, the right of the people to keep and bear Arms, shall not be infringed.

The Second Amendment is the *second* amendment. It follows immediately behind freedom of religion, speech, press, assembly, and petition. It articulates clearly the right to own firearms is an *individual* right. The government does not need the Second Amendment to allow it to own weapons. The Bill of Rights was written to allow citizens to do so, which the US Supreme Court affirmed in a 2008 decision (*District of Columbia v. Heller*).[9]

Authoritative governments generally want to control their citizens so they will do what they are told to do. In virtually every case, except in the US, this involves disarming the general population so the authorities can do whatever they want without serious opposition. The push to limit, or eliminate private firearm ownership is nearly always couched in terms of the public interest, to make it more acceptable to citizens. This is the reason the founders put the amendment in second place on the list. They knew it was vitally important. After all, if the colonists had been without weapons, there would have been no revolution. The British made a concerted effort to keep firearms and power out of the hands of the colonists prior to the Declaration of Independence. This effort was obviously unsuccessful. The battles of Concord and Lexington in April of 1775, which ignited the American revolution, were precipitated due to a British effort to capture arms and munitions in the hands of the colonials.[10]

Throughout history, despotic governments have disarmed their citizenry as a means of maintaining power without significant dissent.

Remember, it is only the law-abiding citizen who will actually comply with firearms laws. Criminals obviously don't care much for laws and would know the population was disarmed, thereby giving them an advantage. Law-abiding citizens are the very ones who need to own firearms, if they desire, for their own defense and for the national defense in a national emergency.

AMENDMENT III

> No Soldier shall, in time of peace be quartered in any
> house, without the consent of the Owner, nor in time
> of war, but in a manner to be prescribed by law.

The colonists were exasperated with the British quartering officers and soldiers on private property and sometimes even in citizens' homes. This occurred in spite of the fact that the British Parliament had passed the Quartering Act of 1765, which stated British troops were not to be quartered in private homes.[11] The act stated that troops were to be quartered in barracks, and when those were not adequate, they could be quartered in public houses and inns at the expense of colonial legislatures.

In addition, the colonists were none too happy that a peacetime army was in the colonies to begin with. All of this continued to remind the colonials they were subject to the Crown. It is also an important reminder today that *private* property is an important element of freedom. It is clear the colonists and the founders thought it to be essential to a free society. What is yours is *yours*. It is not mine. It is also not the government's; it is *yours*.

The Judeo-Christian position on private property is also clear, as the eighth Commandment in Exodus 20:15 prohibits the theft of people's property: "Thou shalt not steal." The apostle Paul echoed this precept in Ephesians 4:28 when he penned: "Anyone who has been stealing must steal no longer, but must work, doing something useful with their own hands, that they may have something to share with those in need."[12] It is also important to note that the sharing with the one that has a need is voluntary.

Private property is a powerful hallmark of freedom. If a government or other group or organization can simply appropriate your possessions without due process and just compensation, then where is your freedom?

AMENDMENT IV

> The right of the people to be secure in their persons, houses, papers, and effects, against unreasonable searches and seizures, shall not be violated, and no Warrants shall issue, but upon probable cause, supported by Oath or affirmation, and particularly describing the place to be searched, and the persons or things to be seized.

We can all recall movies or documentaries where the authorities have broken down doors to private homes and run roughshod over the residents, sometimes even damaging the inside of the home in the process. The colonists were unfortunately quite familiar with this practice, and they wanted no part of it. While it is possible to list several reasonable-sounding arguments for no-knock warrants, the Fourth Amendment would seem to prohibit such behavior on the part of authorities. These types of warrants are dangerous for the officers who carry them out as well as the private citizens who are the subjects of such warrants. Both innocent citizens and law officers have been killed and injured as a result of no-knock warrants.

> Of all tyrannies, a tyranny sincerely exercised for the good of its victims may be the most oppressive.[13] (C.S. Lewis)

Officials can persuasively come up with a rationale that supports freedom-destroying activities. Authorities usually take the position that it is for *the public good.* However, this is where the Constitution comes in. If the Constitution clearly states government cannot do a certain thing, then the activity is illegal. The Bill of Rights is not a list of suggestions. It is the Bill of *Rights.* It is an addition to the Constitution to make the rights of the citizens crystal clear. These rights must be preserved if we are to remain a free society.

AMENDMENT V

> No person shall be held to answer for a capital, or otherwise infamous crime, unless on a presentment or indictment of a Grand Jury, except in cases arising in the land or naval forces, or in the Militia, when in actual service in time of War or public danger; nor shall any person be subject for the same offence to be twice put in jeopardy of life and limb; nor shall be compelled in any criminal case to be a witness against himself, nor be deprived of life, liberty, or property, without due process of law; nor shall private property be taken for public use, without just compensation.

Most of us have heard of the Fifth Amendment in relation to testimony under oath. This is where defendants "plead the Fifth" so they will not have to testify against themselves. This is a Constitutional protection. However, this amendment offers much more in the way of protection for a citizen. It protects persons from any deprivation of life, liberty, or property without due process. Our government cannot just take our property, limit our liberty, or scoop us up and take us to jail without due process. In addition, authorities cannot take property without just compensation.

It has always been my opinion that the inheritance tax is a direct violation of the Fifth Amendment because it takes private property without just compensation. It is important to realize that the average citizen can be powerless against government. We have all heard the old saying: "You can't fight city hall." This is where the Constitution comes in. The clear language of the Fifth Amendment provides legal protection from any overreach or abuse of power.

The acquisition of property for needed roadways and other government infrastructure is allowed by the Fifth Amendment. However, due process must occur, and just compensation must be provided to the person or entity whose property is acquired. Government cannot just take your property for free simply because it has the power. It has happened in other countries, but it should not happen in the United States.

The Fifth Amendment is another strong statement regarding the importance of due process and the value of private property rights to freedom.

AMENDMENT VI

> In all criminal prosecutions, the accused shall enjoy the right to a speedy and public trial, by an impartial jury of the State and district wherein the crime shall have been committed; which district shall have been previously ascertained by law, and to be informed of the nature and cause of the accusation; to be confronted with the witnesses against him; to have compulsory process for obtaining witnesses in his favor, and to have the assistance of counsel for his defense.

The Sixth Amendment provides for a speedy trial, which would reduce the anxiety and expense of the lengthy process currently played out in the US every day. An efficient system of justice is essential for an orderly and productive society. Legal issues must be adjudicated fairly and quickly, or society and economy will be harmed.

Citizens frequently must defend themselves from government action and incur gigantic legal bills in the process. There is something wrong with this picture when you read the Sixth Amendment. Governments have virtually unlimited resources, but private citizens do not. The amendment calls specifically for "a speedy and public trial." This has not been the case in the US in recent years. The legal system needs to be reformed and supplied with the resources to ensure that the Sixth Amendment represents the way the legal system actually works. The US spends billions of dollars on all sorts of less important projects but cannot seem to make the Sixth Amendment a reality. We need a reordering of our priorities.

AMENDMENT VII

> In suits at common law, where the value in controversy exceeds twenty dollars, the right of trial by jury shall be preserved, and no fact tried by a jury, shall be otherwise re-examined in any Court of the United States, than according to the rules of the common law.

Although the twenty dollars would need to be adjusted for inflation, the right to a trial by jury is a time-honored American tradition. The founders witnessed full well the abuses that can occur when a legal system dishes out penalties without any full public review. They did not want to see that happen in the new republic. Their design included a jury to hear and review the evidence and help ensure justice was done. It is not perfect, because we are not perfect, but it is a lot better than putting the whole decision in the hands of a particular judge.

AMENDMENT VIII

> Excessive bail shall not be required, nor excessive fines imposed, nor cruel and unusual punishments inflicted.

A defendant is protected from inappropriate treatment when apprehended after being accused of some infraction of the law. Holding individuals without bail or requiring excessive bail amounts limits the rights of a citizen to be free while the issue is being settled legally. Defendants are provided legal protection from being subjected to cruel and unusual punishment. Certainly, some individuals need to be incarcerated due to the nature of the accusation, but this should not be the normal situation. This is yet another reminder the US Constitution seems to err on the side of the individual rather than the government.

AMENDMENT IX

> The enumeration in the Constitution of certain rights shall not be construed to deny or disparage others retained by the people.

The Ninth Amendment reminds us there are other rights and privileges citizens should enjoy that are not specifically enumerated or spelled out in the Constitution. This addresses the argument by some that if the Constitution does not specifically give citizens a particular right, then they don't have it. Not so!

Governments always seem to want to expand their authority because those running governments think they must respond to almost any problem. If not limited, government can become the be-all and end-all. The Ninth Amendment limits this condition by specifically stating that if a right is not listed in the Constitution, it belongs to the people.

AMENDMENT X

> The powers not delegated to the United States by the Constitution, nor prohibited by it to the States, are reserved to the States respectively, or to the people.

We are the United States of America, not the National Republic of America. Individual US states have sovereign rights. The states have the right to be different, and that is a good thing. During the COVID-19 pandemic, we observed how vastly different state policies produced dramatically different results. Some state policies included near-total lockdowns in 2020 and 2021, severely damaging their economies in the process. Other states limited the breadth and scope of any shutdowns and avoided such poor results. After the fact, it is reasonable to review various state policies and analyze which ones produced the more effective results in preparation for a future event.

The sovereign power of the states serves as a check on the power of the central government. It seems to be a natural progression of central governments to want all citizens to be subject to the same rules and regulations and to usurp the authority of individual states. These tendencies are seen every day in the national news. Those who desire to wield power do not like deviations from their vision of how life ought to be. They want everyone to march to the beat of the same drummer, and they want to be the drummer.

The individuality of the states provides the opportunity for different and unique approaches to challenges. This creates the unmatched, freedom-fueled economic vitality generated by the United States. Milton Friedman said it best: "The greatest threat to freedom is a concentration of power."[14] That power can be concentrated in the hands of powerful businesses or in the hands of a large central government, or both. The antitrust laws were designed to limit the power of business monopolists, but it remains up to the voters and the US Constitution to limit the power of central government. It has always amused me to hear leaders of big government railing about the abuses of big business.

Patrick Henry, in 1775 leading up to the Revolutionary War, courageously declared: "Give me liberty or give me death."[15] He meant it. John Adams, in a 1775 letter to his wife, Abigail, penned: "A constitution of government once changed from freedom, can never be restored. Liberty, once lost, is lost forever."[16]

These powerful and relevant words should echo in our memory as we observe the internal assaults on freedom here in the United States—a nation shining a beacon of freedom around the globe for nearly 250 years. If the United States is not a light for freedom, what nation will be? We must maintain our faithfulness to the Constitution and to the principles of freedom it enumerates. The world needs our example. As Thomas Jefferson stated:

> I hope and firmly believe that the whole world will sooner or later feel benefit from the issue of our assertions of the rights of man.[17]

Why do so many people desire to come to the US both legally and illegally? It is because America is different. To many, America is an idea. That idea stands for freedom, and the whole world knows it. Freedom is a magnet that draws people to it. Freedom produces prosperity, and the people of the world can see this too. It is a powerful combination we need to preserve, protect, and defend. The bottom line is this: *freedom is the essential element.*

CHAPTER 2

ADAM SMITH: THE FATHER OF CAPITALISM

Outside of those who have taken a course in economics, most US citizens are not familiar with a titan of economic theory who holds an apt title: The Father of Capitalism. Some even call him the Father of Economics.

Adam Smith, born in Kirkcaldy, Fife, Scotland, in 1723, was a philosopher and economist known primarily for his magnum opus: *An Inquiry into the Nature and Causes of the Wealth of Nations.* In general use, this publication is referred to as *The Wealth of Nations.* Intriguingly, the publication of this seminal work occurred in 1776, the same year as the Declaration of Independence.

Smith introduced the concept of the "Invisible Hand," referring to self-interest as a powerful guiding principle in a capitalist system. It is important to differentiate self-interest from greed. We all exercise self-interest every day in myriad ways. If we decide to obey a stoplight, we are most probably thinking of our own self-interest. If we run the light, we are risking injury, even death, or a hefty fine, none of which would be in our best interest. These are not decisions based on greed. They are based on self-interest.

Students in my classes over the years were not there because they were greedy. They were there seeking a better and more prosperous life, which was in their self-interest. They did not intend to promote the national interest. But in the process, that is *exactly* what they were doing as they became part of a more productive workforce, which does promote the national interest.

> It is not from the benevolence of the butcher, the brewer, or the baker that we expect our dinner, but from their regard to their own interest.[1] (Adam Smith)

Elon Musk, during the dark days of the pandemic in 2020, articulated the following statement: "If you don't make stuff, there's no stuff."[2] This declaration was a timely and powerful reminder that the productive efforts of the population are what generates the standard of living the United States is known for. It is not created by some government office. It is created by people producing stuff. Musk reminded us that a national shutdown means *there won't be any stuff.* Because a number of state governments responded to the pandemic with extended shutdowns, the result included the harsh reality of supply-chain disruptions and empty shelves. Self-interest and commonsense policies would have kept the economy humming through the pandemic, but government (particularly at the state level) deemed it otherwise. On December 28, 2021, in the midst of continuing debates regarding pandemic-driven government policies, I tweeted the following message: "Those critical of supply-side economics are getting a vivid reality check. Supply matters. When there is not enough stuff, the price goes up. Shutdowns destroy supply."

Now a bank robber might decide it is in their self-interest to rob a bank. However, this illegal and dangerous activity could lead to very bad personal results. It would also *not* be in the national interest. This is where an efficient and fair system of justice and a competent law enforcement process come into play. Self-interest, practiced within the constraints of commonsense laws and regulations, is powerfully productive. If the bank robber determined the risk was too high, perhaps this energy might be directed toward a legal and productive activity.

Channeled in the right direction, self-interest can be a powerful economic motivator. A strong sense of morality and honesty are imperative. An efficient system of justice is a vitally important component. And a respect for the rule of law is a primary prerequisite for a powerful economy.

> Our Constitution was made only for a moral and religious people. It is wholly inadequate to the government of any other.[3] (John Adams, second US President)

The Merriam-Webster Dictionary defines greed as: "An excessive and selfish desire for more of something (such as money) than is needed." Self-interest is not greed. It is commonsense and perfectly justifiable. It makes the world go around as we get out of bed in the morning and pursue productive activities. It is amazing that individuals want to criticize others for being greedy but never want to describe their own activities in a like manner.

> Every individual ... neither intends to promote the public interest, nor knows how much he is promoting it ... he intends only his own security; and by directing that industry in such a manner as its produce may be of the greatest value, he intends only his own gain, and he is in this, as in many other cases, led by an invisible hand to promote an end which was no part of his intention.[4] (Adam Smith)

Smith brilliantly understood that the national interest is enhanced when individuals promote their own self-interest, within the rule of law. Millions of citizens, free to promote their own self-interest each day, simultaneously promote the national interest. Any impediment to this opportunity such as discrimination, oppressive taxes, or onerous regulations hampers individual pursuits, restrains total national production, and reduces the average standard of living for any nation.

A capitalist system can exist and be highly productive with little government guidance or interference. We know this because prior to the Great Depression, the US federal government was quite small. Even so, the United States, with largely unfettered capitalism, developed to the point that its military strength helped put an end to World War I. By 1920, the US had emerged as a prime player on the world economic and military stage.

In fact, nations with large and meddlesome central governments typically have lethargic economies. These realities lend validity to Adam Smith's assertion that capitalism is a powerful antidote to disappointing economic growth. Over and over, year after year, countries showcasing the highest levels of economic freedom outperform those with less freedom.

The Cato Institute created the Human Freedom Index measuring personal, civic, and economic freedom across the world. The 2021 ranking included the following:[5]

1. Switzerland
2. New Zealand
3. Denmark
4. Estonia
5. Ireland
6. Canada and Finland (tied)
7. Australia
8. Sweden
9. Luxembourg

In recent years Hong Kong was consistently listed within the top three regarding human freedom. But no longer. The transfer of control from the United Kingdom to the People's Republic of China moved the Hong Kong environment from freedom to repression.

The United States tied with Germany and Japan for fifteenth place. According to the Cato Institute, countries in the top quartile of freedom enjoy a significantly higher average per capita income ($48,748) than those in other quartiles, and the average per capita income in the least-free quartile is $11,259. Some of the lowest-ranked countries on the list include Mexico (93), Turkey (139), Saudi Arabia (155), Iran (160), Venezuela (164), and Syria (165).[6] Clearly, the level of economic prosperity is related to the level of freedom in a nation. The evidence shows that freedom plays a huge role in economic well-being.

In addition to advocating for freedom in domestic exchange, Adam Smith strongly promoted free international trade. He reasoned that individual nations should produce what they are best at producing and then trade that product with other nations skilled at producing other things. He proclaimed total world production would be greater than if each nation attempted to be self-sufficient.

Smith's philosophy broke with the mercantilist mentality popular during his day. The Oxford English Dictionary defines mercantilism as "the economic theory that a nation's wealth, especially its ability to amass bullion, is increased by a favorable balance of trade, and that a government should encourage such a balance by promoting exports (especially of manufactured goods) and restricting imports."[7]

Mercantilism, also masquerading as protectionism, damages a nation's economy because it aims to limit imports. Imports generally occur when another nation is better at producing something than we are. If we limit these imports through tariffs or import quotas, we are actually protecting our own domestic industry. *It sounds good*, but the result is normally higher prices for everything we protect. Those nations affected then have less ability to buy our products, reducing our level of exports and damaging certain domestic industries. This cat and mouse game can produce retaliation on the part of our trading partners, who then levy tariffs and quotas on our exported goods. The result? Everyone pays more.

This is exactly what happened during the Great Depression with the disastrous Smoot-Hawley Tariff Act of 1930. As the story goes, more than a thousand economists signed a petition pleading with President Hoover not to sign the act into law. To the detriment of the country, he ignored their request and signed the bill anyway. The act wreaked havoc by raising tariffs on thousands of imported goods, igniting a tariff fight with trading partners, and suffocating international trade.[8] Most economists agree the Smoot-Hawley Tariff Act worsened the Depression both in the US and abroad. President Hoover should have listened to the economists; after all, when do a thousand economists ever agree on anything? Former Utah governor, ambassador, and businessman Jon Huntsman Jr. left no doubt where he stands on the process of international trade.

> When America closes its doors, so does everybody else. We are the primary engine of growth in the world, and we are the only beacon of free trade left, and open markets.[9] (Jon Huntsman, Jr.)

Americans are better off today because of competition from foreign automobile producers. The competition for customers makes our domestic producers create better vehicles with a more competitive and consumer-friendly sticker price. Competition can be painful, but it makes us better. The consumer is the beneficiary. In fact, in the US today, it is interesting to determine where your automobile was manufactured. You may own a car made by an American company that was manufactured in China. By the same token, you may own a car made by a foreign producer that was manufactured in Alabama. With free trade, the marketplace determines the best method and place of manufacture. The consumer is the beneficiary, and we at home must be competitive.

> It is the maxim of every prudent master of a family, never to attempt to make at home what it will cost him more to make than to buy. The tailor does not attempt to make his own shoes but buys them from the shoemaker. The shoemaker does not attempt to make his own clothes, but employs a tailor.
>
> What is prudence in the conduct of every private family, can scarce be folly in that of a great kingdom.[10]
> (Adam Smith)

What Smith is spelling out is the value of trading with others to maximize our own economic well-being. It makes as little sense for a farmer to try to make an automobile as it makes for the autoworker to grow soybeans. It is reasonable to make what we make well and efficiently and to trade for those products others make well and efficiently. Without government restraints, this is just how things will work out. However, governments can get involved, for all sorts of high-sounding reasons, and frustrate both domestic and international trade.

Borrowing a page from Adam Smith, our founders prohibited states from enacting tariffs on other states. What brilliance! In the predawn of this country, some states did choose to enact tariffs on goods and products coming in from other states. Can you even imagine? Governor George Clinton in New York led the way by laying an "import" tariff on agriculture products from New Jersey and lumber from Connecticut.[11] These decisions resulted in bitter interstate feuds and trade disputes. Political leaders worried that tensions between the states could lead to civil war as the young country wrestled with important questions of state and national authority. Fortunately, the future treasury secretary Alexander Hamilton vocalized his ardent opposition to state-to-state tariffs and championed a national conversation that contributed in large part to the creation of a central government with the sole authority to enact trade policy. The important thing now is for central government to enact *wise* trade policy.

What would it be like in the United States today had each state retained the power to levy tariffs on products made in other states? It would be an economic calamity. Would we be (or ever have been) the *United* States? And for the consumer, everything would cost more to account for the collection of taxes at the state border. Free trade among and between the states is and has been an important factor in our economic success and prosperity. It is interesting that the European Union has adopted the same principle; it's just that they discovered this principle about two hundred years after our founders did. *The US is the largest free-trade zone in the world*, and we want to keep it this way.

Article 1, Section 10, clause 2 (referred to as the Import-Export clause) of the US Constitution states: "No state shall, without the Consent of Congress lay any imposts or duties on imports or exports, except what may be absolutely necessary for executing its inspection laws: and the net produce of all duties and imposts, laid by any State on imports or exports, shall be for the use of the Treasury of the United States; and all such laws shall be subject to the revision and control of the Congress."[12]

So there it is, a free trade zone for all 50 states. Pure economic brilliance. Every state must compete or be left behind. It cannot pass laws to favor itself. The citizen is the beneficiary of this level economic playing field. It helps explain why and how the US turned into an economic juggernaut. Goods and services flow freely and without restriction among all the states, and this reality helped create one of the world's most powerful and efficient economies.

Few of us are completely thrilled or genuinely excited about strong competition because it makes us work harder and better. However, in sports, business, commerce, the arts, and countless other areas, competition makes us strive to be better. Capitalism does that naturally. Competition challenges us to push ourselves, and the invisible hand of self-interest drives us on to higher levels of creativity, innovation, and efficiency. A nation must do the same. Adam Smith made this clear, and he was right. In the US, Alexander Hamilton echoed these sentiments with his unapologetic support for free trade, open markets, and Adam Smith's "invisible hand."[13]

Freedom is just *better*. Citizens are happier, production is enhanced, and there is no need for a complex government plan to tell us how the economy is supposed to work. Smith wanted to see a free market create the economic prosperity of which it is capable. It's sort of like a good football game. We must have rules, but the referees don't get to call the plays. If they did, the game would be much different. They also do not determine who gets to play the game; that is up to the coach. Coaches who do a poor job get replaced. Players who don't perform get benched. That's just the way it is. Competition is tough, but it produces extraordinary results in personal and national economies just as it does in sports.

There always have been and always will be those who want to limit individual freedom, and they will come up with all sorts of fancy-sounding arguments as to why this should be. However, repeatedly, history proves there is a price for such limitations, and that price is both freedom and prosperity. Smith is not called the Father of Capitalism for nothing. He is called the Father of Capitalism because he deserves the title.

CHAPTER 3

KARL MARX: THE FATHER OF COMMUNISM

KARL MARX WAS A NINETEENTH-CENTURY GERMAN PHILOSOPHER-economist. Most know him best as the author, with Friedrich Engels, of *The Communist Manifesto* published in 1848 and consider him to be the Father of Communism.[1] Marx espoused a central theme, that capitalism exploits the worker and must be replaced.

> Capitalist production, therefore, develops technology,
> and the combining together of various processes into
> a social whole, only by sapping the original sources
> of all wealth, the soil and the laborer.[2] (Karl Marx)

Marx asserted that societies naturally engendered class conflict between the bourgeoisie, who controlled the means of production, and the proletariat who provided the means of production through their labor. Marx believed this conflict would eventually lead to the destruction and replacement of the capitalist system by a more equitable socialist system. He believed the proletariat should carry out revolutions to bring down the bourgeoisie and usher in a new order. This is exactly what happened in Russia in 1917 and later in China after World War II. There were even those in the United States in the

1930s who thought the Great Depression meant capitalism had failed and the ideas of Marx were sound.

> The proletarians have nothing to lose but their chains.
> They have a world to win.[3] (Karl Marx)

My summary of the basic tenets of Marxism includes the following:

- The population of the world is split primarily into two groups of people.
- These two groups are those who control the levers of production and those who provide the labor that creates the production.
- Class conflict between these groups will occur naturally.
- Workers will eventually realize their exploitation and revolt to take over the means of production.
- The replacement for capitalism will be a socialist state.

The collapse of the Russian government of Tsar Nicholas II in 1917 seemed to indicate that maybe Marx was correct. Vladimir Lenin became the first head of the new communist government and used force and ruthless cruelty to solidify power and control in the new state until his death in 1924. As a Marxist, Lenin developed his own personal brand of communism known as Leninism.[4] Joseph Stalin followed Lenin and ruled with an iron hand until he died in 1953. The Soviet Union survived for a total of seventy-four years until its collapse in 1991.

> The proletariat will use its political supremacy to wrest, by degrees, all capital from the bourgeoisie; to centralize all instruments of production in the hands of the State, i.e., of the proletariat organized as the ruling class; and to increase the total productive forces as rapidly as possible.[5] (The Communist Manifesto)

One of the most significant limitations of communism is that the efficiency and level of production is low. It is hard to get workers to strive for the best when everything is collective. It is private enterprise where employees can see that their efforts can produce personal benefits where production and efficiency are at their greatest. The late Dr. Scott Boaz, a friend, colleague, economist, and Russian linguist, used to tell his students the following joke about communism in the USSR. He said he was observing some Russian workers who seemed to be moving at a snail's pace in their daily activities. He asked one of them why they were working so slow. The response: "Well, we pretend to work, and they pretend to pay us."

That about sums it up. Few incentives existed in the USSR for good or exceptional results. There were certainly penalties for not meeting the state goals and metrics, but penalties are very different from incentives. The leaders of the USSR relied on the gun and the gulag to keep everyone in order.

It seems ironic that Marx promoted the idea that a communist revolution would return to the working individual the fruits of their production. The reality has been just the opposite. In practice, the fruits of labor are transferred to those in positions of power within the communist power structure, and the benefits to the workers have turned out to be minimal. It is those leaders of the party and the military who have benefited most, and the worker has been left behind.

I vividly remember boarding a Moscow train in 1991 to travel 439 miles to Leningrad, now St. Petersburg. As we departed the somber but modern city of Moscow, we witnessed a stark reality; much of the rest of the country looked third world. Some of the villages we passed through mirrored scenes from the movie *Doctor Zhivago*, set during the time of the Russian Revolution. Everywhere it has been tried, and I mean everywhere, the communist system simply has not lived up to its promises.

After we arrived in St. Petersburg, our tour guide directed our gaze across the Neva River to a vintage World War I warship moored at the dock with the Soviet flag still flying from the mast. She would have never made the following statement without knowing that the old USSR was collapsing. She pointed to the ship and said, "That is the cruiser *Aurora* that fired a blank shot in 1917 to signal the beginning of the October Russian Revolution. We refer to this vessel as the most powerful ship in the Soviet navy: one blank shot followed by seventy-four years of destruction." This is the exact length of the brutal communist experiment in Russia from 1917 to 1991, seventy-four years.

The greatly heralded communistic system failed to compete with or even remotely keep up with capitalism. Everywhere it is applied, government control of an economy destroys freedom, personal initiative, choice, and entrepreneurship. These are the exact qualities capitalism allows to run free, resulting in a vibrant, productive, and prosperous economy.

In the summer of 1990, my daughter Beth Anne received an unexpected phone call from the president of her university, Ouachita Baptist University, inviting her to have an exchange student from the USSR as a roommate for the upcoming school year. Having grown up during the reality of the Cold War (and with a free-market economist for a dad), Beth Anne had heard many examples of the economic contrasts between the United States and the USSR. As school launched that fall, she drove from Arkadelphia to the Little Rock airport with five other OBU students to await the arrival of their Soviet roommates as the plane touched down in Arkansas. What began that night was a lifelong friendship with a brilliant young student named Alia from Kazakhstan, who later became an American citizen.

That experience produced many highlights, and Beth Anne still speaks about the impact of spending a semester with a roommate who grew up under the harsh economic realities of communism. Everyday conveniences, freedoms, and choices that were "normal routine" here in the US were immediately seen through the eyes of someone who had a completely different experience living under the mantle of communism in the Soviet Union. Beth Anne spoke of the first time the two of them popped into the local Walmart and how she will never forget the look of sheer awe, amazement, and joy on her roommate's face as she saw rows and rows of shelves, stocked full and brimming with countless items, products, and options. So many choices, and affordable at that! Free enterprise at its best, and a poignant contrast to the scarcity and rampant shortages to which people living in the USSR had grown accustomed.

Under communism, the free market still exists (sort of); it's just that it isn't "free." But it is real. It is *underground.* It has a name—the Black Market. Wherever you find communism and the suppression of a *truly* free market, you will undoubtedly find this underground economy where goods and services are still traded, exchanged, bought, and sold, but invisibly.

While in Moscow (1991), with the old system still in place, I saw firsthand how capitalism is hard to keep down and under control. Every time our group unloaded from the bus, cars drove up and young men jumped out and popped the trunks of their cars to hawk all sorts of merchandise. Capitalism just happens. It is as natural as eating ice cream. It is part of human nature to want to do good for oneself. These individuals were simply trying to make a buck with a careful eye out for the authorities. They would take rubles or dollars. Although as one entrepreneur told me as I handed him some dollars: "Be careful, this is a crazy country."

Fast forward to the future. We see China, a communist nation, striving to dethrone the United States as the number one military and economic power in the world. Other than minor players like Cuba and North Korea, China is the sole remaining major communist country. However, China's version of communism is not pure communism. It is a concoction of communism, fascism, and capitalism. Ironically, in the late 1970s under Deng Xiaoping, China adopted a variety of capitalist policies that unleashed a new level of productivity in the nation. China is certainly a totalitarian state, but it is taking on more of the characteristics of a fascist rather than a communist state. A fascist state attempts to combine a one-party system of complete control with strong elements of capitalism, partially controlled (but not owned) by the state. The Chinese Communist Party has begun to realize private enterprise is dramatically more productive and competitive than state-run enterprises.

In the summer of 2021, I interviewed my friend and colleague Dr. Limount Zhao about his experience growing up in Communist China under Mao Zedong. He lived there until he was twenty-eight and then immigrated to the United States. Dr. Zhao earned a PhD in finance from Mississippi State University and then came to teach at Southern Arkansas University. Below are excerpts from this interview, which I think you will find fascinating.[6]

> When I was little, we literally didn't have enough food. We had the central planning system. My parents worked hard for the commune. We had a team in our village. There were twelve teams. My parents worked hard, but we just didn't have enough food.
>
> In 1978, the communists started reforms and peasants started to have their own land. I could quickly, immediately, see the difference. By 1981, my parents started to have enough food. We had our first house.
>
> We (before the changes) had grain rationing. We ate lots of rice. I did not eat an apple until I was eleven or twelve years old. When the system changed, we started to have food. My family was given four or five acres. My parents started to raise some pigs. In 1987,

> I was able to go to college. Things just started to get better and better. (Limount Zhao)

No matter how hard authoritarian governments try, it seems state-run enterprises cannot even provide the basics and certainly cannot compete with capitalism. The seventy-four-year Russian experiment with communism was a colossal failure, and the current communist governments of other nations have standards of living that fall far short of capitalist nations. From Dr. Zhao's comments above, it is clear the Maoist version of communism could not even meet the basic nutritional needs of the population. China certainly tried Mao's version of communism. It just did not work. Communist countries such as North Korea and Cuba struggle to provide the necessities of life, and their citizens suffer. Economic data reveal the contrast between the two systems, but all you need to do is think about the economic and social differences between North Korea and South Korea or Cuba and Miami, to understand the economic consequences of autocratic socialism.

Marx crafted intriguing utopian ideas, but they just do not work in the real world. Top-down government planning and direction can sound good. "Just give us the power, and we will accomplish great and wonderful things," advocates say. But when you hear these statements, think about the years of destruction and suffering the citizens of the former USSR experienced. Think about the lack of basic foodstuffs in Mao's China with his version of communism. This economic model only works if you are willing to provide enough force to keep everyone in line. If the force is removed, the whole system falls apart, just as it did in the USSR in 1991. Without brute force, Communism cannot survive, and force destroys personal freedom. It also exacts a tremendous human cost.

> The goal of socialism is communism.[7] (Vladimir Lenin)

In the US today, it is concerning to read polls indicating that a significant percentage of college students hold a positive view of socialism. How can this be? History books brim with reports of the meager economic benefits of socialism and the more extreme forms that lead to widespread brutality. Communism and fascism are blights on the human landscape. The results are irrefutable, and the human impact is dismal. Is it that too few of our college professors have had any real-world experience? Are too many unaware of the documentable, brutal experience with communism and fascism that so many have experienced? When we think of the Holocaust, we must also think of fascism. When we think of the gulag, we must also think of communism. These two forms of socialism, as well as less brutal forms, are enemies of freedom.

Karl Marx and Friedrich Engels were the dreamers. Lenin, Mao, Castro, and many others have been the doers. The results have been catastrophic. Even today, we see North Korea's closed and brutal society. We see China's harsh repression of minorities and the constant threatening of Taiwan. The repressive regime in Cuba continues to provide only meager economic results for its citizens. We also need to remember the differences between East and West Germany before the fall of the Berlin Wall. Communism never changes, and it cannot tolerate freedom. It starts out espousing lofty goals and descends quickly into intimidation, suppression, and brutality.

Political power grows out of the barrel of a gun.[8] (Mao Zedong)

In the United States we must not flirt with communism or fascism. It is a dangerous game. Former member nations of the USSR cast off communism and have benefited as a result. World War II freed Europe from fascism. And yet today, free nations seem to be lured toward more government control, which means more socialism. The result: big powerful governments; underperforming economies;

political leaders with too much power; and citizens with too little freedom.

Powerful forces in the US today want to divide our population on the basis of race, gender, and income. This is the same approach Marx advocated when he promoted conflict between the bourgeoisie and the proletariat to achieve his greater socialist goal. It is the idea of dividing and conquering. It is not a new idea, and it often works.

This is not what *E Pluribus Unum* is all about. This official motto of the United States is Latin for: "Out of many, one." We find this inscription on the Great Seal of the nation which was first proposed by Benjamin Franklin, John Adams, and Thomas Jefferson in August of 1776 and adopted by Congress in 1782.[9] This is totally at odds with balkanization (the division of a nation into smaller homogeneous entities). Once divided up, these entities risk susceptibility to radical agendas that promote real and perceived inequities, resulting in an unraveling of national identity and unity. Marxists have used this condition to promote their call for a socialist utopia, appealing to all those who feel aggrieved.

Why don't we ever learn the lessons of history? We can review these tactics with a study of the communist revolutions in Russia, China, and Cuba. However, the result is always the same: initial exhilaration followed by oppression and deprivation. Dividing a nation up and emphasizing the differences enhances the abilities of revolutionaries to accomplish their mission.

Except for the Civil War, the United States has been just that—*united*. Political and social differences certainly exist, but national unity has carried the day. However, this unity must be protected if we are going to continue to prosper. The Marxist playbook is to divide and conquer. After divisions are accomplished, force is applied to create a *mandated* national unity around a communist banner.

> Give me four years to teach the children and the seed I
> have sown will never be uprooted.[10] (Vladimir Lenin)

The schools are a key target where discord and discontent can be sown, intentionally leading to national conflict. If we divide ourselves up into warring camps, we will lose our national unity and purpose. We will also be easy prey to those who wish us harm. It is important to study our history, but assigning blame to current generations for issues of the past does not promote unity. It promotes disunity. Marx and Lenin understood this well. It is important to remember that the bitterness in Germany over its treatment after World War I contributed to the political environment that led to World War II.

One of the keys to national unity is to teach the principles that unite us in our schools and universities. These are not radical ideas; they are freedom and prosperity ideas. This provides a citizenry and workforce that comes from a shared (similar if not identical) appreciation for the history of the nation. At least they know about it. The United States was founded by colonists who desired freedom from the dictates of the British Parliament and King George III. They were willing to sacrifice and risk everything, and they won. Eighty-five years later, others sacrificed during the Civil War to ensure that freedom was expanded to include all citizens. Today, the opportunity to enjoy the fruits of freedom is a beacon attracting people from around the world who come here by the millions to participate in a free society.

John Locke said it well in his *Second Treatise of Government* written in 1690: "Being all equal and independent, no one ought to harm another in his life, health, liberty, or possessions. Men being, as has been said, by nature, all free, equal and independent, no one can be put out of this estate, and subjected to the political power of another, without his own consent."[11] Joseph Carrig noted, in his Introduction to Locke's *Treatise*, that the principles of "individual liberty, the rule of law, government by consent of the people, and the right to private property" are central themes echoed later by not only our founding fathers but also by economists Adam Smith, Friedrich Hayek, and Milton Friedman.[12]

Communism stands in stark conflict with the principles of liberty, rule of law, consent, and private property. Ultimately, communism stands in conflict with freedom. Freedom is a precious thing, and it has many enemies. There are those who want to *explain* to you how your life should be lived, and then they want to *control* how your life is lived. It is fine for them to have an opinion, but when they cross the line and strive to use some sort of institutional power to implement their ideas, freedom suffers. Communism, fascism, and socialism all restrict and suffocate freedom.

President Ronald Reagan articulated it well when he said, "How do you tell a Communist? Well, it's someone who reads Marx and Lenin. And how do you tell an anti-Communist? It's someone who understands Marx and Lenin."[13] As William F. Buckley aptly stated in 1995 following the fall of the Iron Curtain, "What was wrong with communism wasn't aberrant leadership, it was communism."[14]

CHAPTER 4

MILTON FRIEDMAN: CHAMPION OF THE FREEDOM TO CHOOSE

IN THE 1980s, I ASKED ONE OF MY OUTSTANDING STUDENTS, MICHELE Belmont, to write an essay for the Americanism Educational League essay national competition. Her remarkable paper landed in the top three nationally, resulting in invitations for Michele, my wife Toni, and me to attend an awards banquet in Los Angeles. An added bonus included the news that Nobel Prize winner for economics, Dr. Milton Friedman, would be the keynote speaker for the event. Naturally, we accepted and flew off to Los Angeles. Previously, I had heard Professor Friedman speak at Harding University in Arkansas and was wholly impressed with the way he artfully presented economic concepts in a bold, engaging, and understandable way.

On the flight out, visiting with Michele, I asked her what year she graduated from high school. She looked at me and said she did not have a high school diploma. Surprised, I asked her why not. She explained she only had one course to take in high school her senior year, so she just came on to college. A not-surprising decision from such a talented young lady. Michele was free to make that choice and move ahead to pursue her higher education.

At the hotel, Professor Friedman hosted the three finalists and their professors and spouses in his suite prior to the banquet. Dr. Friedman asked each of us to introduce and tell something about ourselves. Of course, we professors and students had some of the predictable things on our résumés. The other two spouses were both in the workforce and had impressive things to say. My wife Toni, who was a full-time homemaker with three kids to look after on our farm, explained this to the group and then followed up with "I was free to choose." Great response! This is what real freedom is all about: the freedom to order our lives according to what we see as best without limitation.

Michele placed second in the essay competition, and it was an outstanding evening. Unexpectedly, Dr. Friedman invited us back up to his suite following the awards ceremony for another visit that lasted until midnight. I could not believe it. We had the opportunity to spend a whole evening with one of the most brilliant individuals I have ever met. We were mesmerized. Over and over, we threw out economic topics for discussion and listened to a fountain of wisdom coming forth.

To say Friedman had an impact on my professional life would be a dramatic understatement. This impact has been repeated for thousands of individuals influenced by his presentations and writings. If you have never read *Free to Choose,* I highly recommend it. Though it was written in 1979, the economic wisdom is extraordinarily relevant today.

Milton Friedman won the Nobel Prize in 1976 for his work in the area of monetary theory and consumption analysis. Friedman was a strong proponent of stable growth in the money supply to create an environment of sound money and low inflation.

He is particularly noted for his analysis of the causes of the Great Depression of the 1930s. Ironically, Congress established the Federal Reserve System in 1913 to "provide the nation with a safer, more flexible, and more stable monetary and financial system."[1] The Federal Reserve was designed to *prevent* economic disasters like the Great Depression. The Fed possessed both the mandate and the power to ensure the nation had an ample supply of money to meet the needs of the economy. Inexcusably, in the case of the Great Depression, the Fed failed miserably in its mission. The citizens in our country suffered greatly as a result.

With the failure of one-third of the nation's banks and a decline in the money supply of roughly one-third, the results were predictable: an economic calamity. It was a bitter and severe decade, and it lasted until World War II put millions in the armed forces and most everyone else in a defense plant or other essential production. According to Friedman, the Depression never should never have happened.

The new Roosevelt administration addressed the problem with broad efforts to create jobs and stimulate demand when the actual (initial) problem was a lack of money. Many parts of the country virtually went back to the barter system to keep commerce moving at all. *There simply was no money.* Those who actually had some cash could buy all sorts of things at bargain prices. The Federal Reserve should have acted and ensured there was enough money in circulation to prevent the level of economic destruction that occurred.

> The Great Depression, like most other periods of severe unemployment, was produced by government mismanagement rather than by any inherent instability of the private economy.[2] (Milton Friedman)

Friedman asserted that the Federal Reserve allowed a recession to become the Great Depression, and then the Roosevelt administration had to try to save us from it. This happens a lot with big government. Governments create poor policies. Poor policies create problems. The same governments then try to take credit for "rescuing" us from the problems that its policies created in the first place.

It happens over and over again. Same formula. Same process. I have always told my students you can never, ever, ever let your banking system fail. But that is exactly what the Federal Reserve did at the beginning of the Great Depression. I do believe we learned our lesson, but at a tremendous cost.

The exact opposite situation occurred during the Carter administration in the late 1970s. The problem at that point was *too much money.* Once again, Friedman was right when he asserted, "Inflation is always and everywhere a monetary phenomenon, it's always and everywhere a result of too much money, of a more rapid increase in the quantity of money than the output."[3] In this case, the Federal Reserve allowed the money supply to expand too rapidly, allowing inflation to get out of hand. For those of us old enough to remember, inflation reached 1.5 percent per month in the fall of 1980. Small wonder that incumbent President Carter was defeated by Ronald Reagan in November of that year.

Friedman's basic position was that the money supply matters. If the money supply is expanded at a faster rate than output, then inflation is going to occur. If inflation gets out of control, then the only solution is to slow the growth of the money supply. The result is higher interest rates, and frequently a recession follows. After inflation comes under control, at some point the money supply can be allowed to grow again. Of course, the Federal Reserve System is in control of the money supply. This is why everyone holds their breath when the current chairman of the Fed (whoever it may be at the time) schedules a press conference. Yes, it is *that* important. The key is for the Federal Reserve to not let things get out of control in the first place. The inflation of 2022-2023 is just another example of inflation getting out of control and then having to be dealt with.

Milton Friedman is known for many other bold proposals, most of which were thirty to forty years ahead of his time. For example, in *Free to Choose,* he advocated educational vouchers to give parents more choice regarding their children's education.[4] Basically, money would follow the student, providing competition and freedom in the K-12 school selection process. Interestingly, this would introduce and reflect the kind of student freedom and competition we see in today's higher education landscape. When competition enters the scene, quality generally goes up, and the whole educational system grows increasingly more receptive to parental objectives and concerns. What we are talking about here is a free market in K-12 education. Schools (public, private, and charter) would compete for students. Parents and students would have choices, much like potential college freshmen have when they consider various colleges and universities they might attend each fall.

> Our goal is to have a system in which every family in the U.S. will be able to choose for itself the school to which its children go. If we had that, a system of free choice, we would also have a system of competition, innovation, which would change the character of education.[5] (Milton Friedman)

In higher education, competition (state scholarships available to all) has not harmed public colleges and universities. What competition has done is create more competitive and innovative institutions of higher learning that are more attentive to students and parents. These institutions court students and invite them to campus for all types of events to try and secure their enrollment.

In a free educational market, school boards and administrators, instead of stonewalling parents and students as some do, would become more responsive. Students would acquire mobility, providing both students and parents with another level of power and choice. This is appropriate. After all, they are the ones paying the freight.

The state of Arizona in 2022 enacted Arizona's Empowerment Scholarship Accounts (ESA) that are open to every K-12 student. Each Arizona child will receive an approximately $6,500 voucher, 90 percent of normal state funding per student, which they can use at virtually any school of their choice.[6] Through this legislation, real competition in the K-12 sphere has been created in Arizona. Arkansas and West Virginia have enacted similar school choice programs. This is not going to ruin public schools. It is going to make them better because they will have to be better to survive. The good schools will prosper, and the poor ones will either change or wither. Competition will see to it. Who are the beneficiaries of this competition? You might have guessed it already—the students.

Friedman's views on bringing competition to education were certainly controversial at the time, as they still are. They were way ahead of his time. But good ideas have a way of finding the light of day, and school choice has become an attractive opportunity for parents and students in search of excellence in education. It was only a matter of time, and the time is now. More and more states are going to introduce competition into their K-12 systems. Freedom and choice are powerful motivators for educators and students alike.

Dr. Friedman was a staunch advocate for freedom in many areas. A self-described libertarian, he nearly always came down on the side of individual freedom. He knew big government is not the answer. The individual is the answer.

> There is only one alternative to free markets, force, some people telling other people what to do.[7] (Milton Friedman)

Freidman was right. Either we make our own decisions, or someone else makes them for us. The more decisions we make for ourselves, the freer we are. If we shift too many decisions to government, we damage and limit freedom for ourselves and our fellow citizens. *Once we cede freedom, it is virtually impossible to get it back.* Just ask the citizens of the Peoples Republic of China (PRC) who overthrew the Republic of China (ROC) and installed Mao Zedong and communism on the mainland. After the communist revolution in 1949, the ROC retreated to Taiwan, where its citizens have prospered.

In this case, the Republic of China (ROC) accurately describes what it actually is. Taiwan is a multiparty democracy. However, this does not sit well with the PRC, which consistently lobs threats and warnings regarding Taiwan. China still claims Taiwan as part of its territory. Despite China's opposition, the island has prospered and is highly ranked in both freedom and economic development. Taiwan is a strong and clear example of what freedom and capitalism can accomplish under the rule of law. However, with the giant communist nation of China just a few miles away, the citizens of the ROC poignantly understand their freedom is always in danger.

Friedman's *Free to Choose* video series was aired on the Public Broadcasting System in 1979 and proved a huge success.[8] If you have never seen it, it is available on the Internet and is still incredibly valuable today. Capitalism is not rocket science. It is basic common sense. However, it seems that common sense *is* rocket science for those who have the big government mindset. Perhaps they need to pay attention to Milton Friedman and his writings and videos. You never know; lightning may strike, and they may discover that the freedom to choose is essential for "Life, Liberty and the pursuit of Happiness."

CHAPTER 5

JOHN MAYNARD KEYNES: THE FATHER OF KEYNESIAN ECONOMICS

Initially educated as a British mathematician, John Maynard Keynes (1883–1946) emerged as one of the most influential economists of the twentieth century, particularly during and after the Great Depression. His ideas became so mainstream they are now known as Keynesian economics.[1]

With the development of the Great Depression, governments around the world searched for a plan to get the wheels of business and industry turning again. International trade withered, unemployment skyrocketed, and economic growth went seriously negative. National economies around the world spiraled into deflation, and many thought capitalism had failed. Keynes's 1936 blockbuster *The General Theory of Employment, Interest and Money* was just the ticket for those who wanted governments to take a larger role in the economic life of nations. Classical economists had long argued the free market would return an economy to full employment due to adjustments to wages and prices. However, Keynes argued that government must utilize fiscal and monetary policy to counteract the unpleasant effects of recessions and depressions. He asserted that when the economy did not have an adequate level of aggregate demand, then government should pursue policies to stimulate demand and move the economy toward full employment. That is exactly what the Roosevelt administration (1933–1945) did to deal with the Depression. Roosevelt's government instituted one federal program after another in a desperate effort to get the US economy moving.[2]

A colleague of mine worked on our university campus during the 1930s to construct what we now call the Greek Theatre. The project was an effort by the National Youth Administration to put money into the pockets of large numbers of unemployed young people. The pay was low, but it was pay, and it kept the wolf away from the door. Initiatives like this and others including the Civilian Conservation Corps and the Public Works Administration aimed to put purchasing power in empty pockets and create something of value.[3] Many of the bridges and highways we still use today were initially constructed during the Depression. Some of these programs were declared unconstitutional, but many others remained and formed the core efforts to revitalize the economy.

Due to large-scale bank failures, the money supply shrank so significantly that the demand for goods and services dramatically declined. Many Americans lost everything. Money was very scarce. My father was in college at the time, and his parents were farmers. His dad sent him a short note reading as follows: "Dear Curt: There is no money. Be careful. Dad." That's the way it was. *There was no money.* If you have no money, you can't buy things. The national dollar Gross Domestic Product declined by a catastrophic 45 percent between 1929 and 1933 ($104.6 to $57.2 billion).[4] It seemed to many that the world as they had known it was ending.

It was a demand shock, and something had to be done. But the nation had no experience with such a situation. To achieve a quick solution, it would have taken a massive "put money in people's pockets" initiative. It would also have taken the recovery of the lost banks and their deposits. Economists know you don't let the banks fail. Yet, that is precisely what we did. This was monetary policy run amuck. The government also put restrictions on international trade, which just made things worse. What we needed was "helicopter money" and lots of it. The term helicopter money is a reference to dropping money out of helicopters to have an instant effect on purchasing power. In other words, we needed a massive (and quick) infusion of purchasing power injected into the economy. It did not happen.

The Keynesian economics that blossomed during the Depression also charged boldly into the 1950s, 60s, and 70s. Interestingly enough, this coincided with many economists questioning the wisdom of the large-scale role the central government was playing in the economy at the time. It also seemed that the concentration primarily on the level of demand in the economy was tending to increase prices.

President Nixon was forced to resign in 1974 due to the Watergate scandal, and his vice president, Gerald Ford, became president. Inflation swelled while the rate of economic growth stagnated. Americans coined the term "stagflation" to describe the situation.[5] President Ford decided to fight inflation with a Whip Inflation Now (WIN) program in 1974 and encouraged citizens to curb their spending habits and save more money to reduce inflation.[6] He declared inflation "Public Enemy Number One" and asked citizens to sign a pledge and wear WIN buttons as a visible show of support.

The following is the WIN pledge announced by President Ford in the White House's Cabinet Room on November 13, 1974. If you mailed the pledge form to the president, you received a WIN button in return.

Consumers:

> I pledge to my fellow citizens that I will buy, when possible, only those products and services priced at or below present levels. I also promise to conserve energy and I urge others to sign this pledge.

Businessmen and Businesswomen:

I pledge to my customers that to the very best of my ability I will hold or reduce prices and will buy whenever possible from those who have pledged to do the same. I also pledge to be an energy saver. This signed pledge is evidence of my participation in, and support of, the WIN Program.

Workers:

I pledge that I—through my union—will join with my fellow workers and my employer in seeking ways to conserve energy and eliminate waste on the job. I also promise to urge others to sign this pledge.[7]

Most economists recognize that a nation cannot tame inflation with a mere public relations campaign. President Ford's WIN effort is generally considered a serious political blunder and failure that did little to reduce the rate of inflation. In the 1976 presidential election two years later, Georgia Governor Jimmy Carter defeated President Ford, primarily due to a lackluster economy. However, inflationary pressures continued during Carter's term and reached a peak in the fall of 1980 when the general level of prices increased at 1½ percent per month (13.5 percent for all of 1980).[8]

California Governor Ronald Reagan, in his campaign against President Carter that fall, made a lot of political hay out of the pain the nation's citizens were suffering because of high inflation and interest rates. To attack Carter's economic policies, Reagan coined the term "Misery Index," consisting of the rate of inflation, the rate of interest, and the rate of unemployment all added together.

We learned from Milton Friedman that the primary cause of the Great Depression was too little money. Numerous bank failures meant that money was scarce as hen's teeth. Too *little* money creates deflation, and indeed it did. How did we not realize, during the 1970s, that too *much* money creates inflation and cannot be canceled by a gimmicky national public relations program?

During the 1930s, the Federal Reserve System failed to ensure the national economy had a sufficient level of money to maintain economic growth. Then during the 1970s it allowed the money supply to grow faster than needed for stable economic growth, thus ushering in inflation.

Keynesian economics would have never become popular if the Federal Reserve had done its job and prevented the Depression in the first place. It is another instance of government causing or allowing an event or situation to occur and then adopting massive programs to help save us from the same event. It happens repeatedly where a large central government is present. When a problem presents itself, we too often look to central government for a solution and tell our political leaders to "do something." Too often, that "something" is the *wrong thing*.

Governments are much better at stimulating an economy than slowing one down. Once government programs are in place, they stay there—basically *forever*. The Agricultural Adjustment Act of 1933 was created to deal with the collapse of agricultural prices in the 1930s.[9] Key elements of this Act are still with us today. If you have ever seen the size of the Department of Agriculture building in Washington, DC, you would be instantly aware of just how big a "temporary" government program can grow. Ask a central government to spend money, and it is only too happy to do so. Ask one to reduce spending, and you would think the entire sky is falling.

This is the Achilles' heel of Keynesian economics. Political leaders get excited about increasing government spending and adding new programs. It is painless in the early stages, and it is also particularly attractive when the prospect of reelection comes around.

However, boundless government spending runs into trouble when the chickens come home to roost. It happened during the 1970s when inflation raged, economic growth stagnated, and unemployment reached postwar heights. It took the recession of 1981–82 to slow the economy and wring inflation out of the system. In that case, the Federal Reserve *did* act appropriately with the support of President Reagan. However, the monetary medicine produced a nasty recession with the unemployment rate rising to 10.8 percent in 1982.[10] Reagan led an effort to blend fiscal policy and monetary policy to tame inflation and interest rates and regain a strong rate of economic growth.

Reagan cooperated with Federal Reserve Chairman Paul Volcker to reduce the rate of growth in the money supply. He worked simultaneously with Democrat Speaker of the House Thomas Phillip "Tip" O'Neill Jr. to pass the bipartisan Economic Recovery Tax Act of 1981, reducing personal income tax rates by 25 percent and indexing the tax brackets for inflation.[11] An additional personal income tax rate reduction followed in 1986.[12]

Although a painful recession could not be avoided as monetary policy squeezed inflation out of the economic system, the payoff was dramatic. Reagan's economic approach resulted in a reduction in both interest rates and inflation and led to a strong recovery that propelled him to a landslide win in the 1984 presidential election. Reagan seemed to possess a strong understanding of economics. He certainly put his economics degree from little Eureka College to good use during the 1980s. Except for 1990–91, inflation and interest rates have remained largely under control—until the surge in 2022, which was a direct result of the pandemic shutdowns.

Speaking of shutdowns, the government-led shutdowns in spring 2020 provided a striking example of the application of Keynesian principles. Both national and state shutdowns torpedoed the economy and destroyed trillions of dollars in economic activity. Without the CARES act of $2.2 trillion in stimulus funds, we might surely have experienced an economic catastrophe in the United States and beyond. Without a doubt, we were headed for a second Great Depression.

The cure was pure Keynesian economics. Beginning in the second quarter, private demand withered. The deficit in demand was made up with government spending. *A lot* of government spending. This was classic helicopter money. Remember, it was the federal government's shutdowns followed by lengthy state and local shutdowns that created the catastrophe in the first place. Did no one count the cost of all this? To make up for the lost private demand, the federal government dump-trucked trillions of dollars on the economy.

This is interestingly similar to the Great Depression. In the 1930s, the Federal Reserve recklessly allowed thousands of banks to fail and allowed the money supply to decline. The federal government then embarked on a decade-long effort to replace all this lost demand. The same thing happened in 2020, but with lightning speed. The shutdown hammered demand, which then had to be replaced, and it was, by the central government. The Federal Reserve System then did its job and made sure the US Treasury had plenty of money.

We survived, but the cost was alarming. The federal deficit ballooned to $3.1 trillion in fiscal year 2020 (ending on September 30) and was $2.8 trillion in 2021. Imagine what would have happened to the US economy if the Federal Reserve had not had plenty of dry powder left to provide the funds to the Treasury. The tremendous increase in the federal debt would never have happened if the government, at all levels, had initially showcased more common sense in dealing with the pandemic.

It becomes obvious that carefully considered monetary policy is crucial to prevent all these ups and downs. Milton Friedman believed an economy needed enough money to contribute to sensible economic growth—but not too much. It is also important to distinguish between fiscal policy and monetary policy:

Fiscal Policy	Monetary Policy
The use of a central government's taxing and spending policies to move and keep an economy near full employment.	The management of the money supply to enhance economic growth, but with modest inflation and moderate interest rates.

Keynesians know how to stimulate an economy, but they are less enthusiastic about reducing economic growth to deal with inflation. Keynes came along at just the right time as the Great Depression (worldwide) continued. Keynes provided the Roosevelt administration the justification it needed to develop a wide range of government programs to deal with the issue. President Nixon declared in 1971 that he was "now a Keynesian in economics." However, it was a combination of both fiscal and monetary policy that restored the economic fortunes of the nation in the 1980s.

We economists argue over all of this ad infinitum. What is clear to me is that fiscal and monetary policy can work well together in the theoretical sense. However, the politics of the moment frequently throw commonsense economic policy out the window, and we embark on another wild ride.

Keynes was correct about his primary argument. If there is a dramatic shock to the demand for goods and services in an economy, fiscal stimulus is in order and monetary policy must ensure an adequate amount of money. The problem is shutting the spigot off. This exact phenomenon occurred in March 2021 when Congress passed an additional $1.9 trillion stimulus package—*after* the economy had already reached strong recovery. To top this, the new Biden administration had initially proposed $3.5 trillion in additional spending and a $1.2 trillion infrastructure bill on top of that. Most of this proposed spending fell by the wayside, but we must ask the question: where does it all stop? We have morphed Keynesian economics into Modern Monetary Theory (MMT).

Modern Monetary Theory (which we will discuss in chapter

10) basically says that what the central government borrows simply doesn't matter. The idea is that government is limited in its spending, money creation, and borrowing only by inflation. This is like giving the central government a blank check to borrow and spend whatever it wants. The Achilles' heel is that governments seem to display an unlimited appetite for spending. Without some sort of limit and sensible blending of fiscal and monetary policy, the national debt will head for the stratosphere.

By fall 2021, the additional stimulus plus the effects of the shutdowns were beginning to be felt. The rate of inflation ran in the 5.0 percent range, and supply-chain bottlenecks affected all manner of goods and services.[13] Help-wanted ads popped up everywhere, and whole rows of shelves in some stores were empty. The transportation of goods clogged up with cargo ships stacked up at the nation's harbors due to a lack of truck drivers and dockworkers to move the merchandise. Manufacturers experienced severe shortages of raw materials and parts to feed their production process. A trip to your local auto dealer's lot told the tale. There were hardly any cars on the lot, and numerous auto factories had been shut down due to a shortage of computer chips. All of this was happening at the same time that stimulus payments increased the demand for almost everything.

Many Americans may have heard about supply-side economics but did not really understand it. The bottom line is that the more of a good or service is available, the more reasonable the price. Therefore, anything affecting the supply of something is going to affect the price. Everything else remaining equal, if the supply is reduced, the price will go up; and if the supply is increased, the price will go down. That is the way markets work, and it is supported by common sense.

The pandemic created a demand shock which was addressed through trillions of dollars of stimulus money injected into the economy. The good thing about the CARES act is that most of the money went *directly into people's pockets*. It was not a long list of national programs that would have taken time to set up and get going.

This stimulus was direct, it was fast, and it worked. The reaction to the pandemic (shutdowns) also created a supply shock that raised prices and created inflation. We stimulated demand at the same time the shutdowns hammered the supply chain. The result? All sorts of shortages. All of this was self-inflicted and need never have happened. We did this to ourselves and suffered the consequences. We cannot afford to do this again.

The level of national demand is important, the monetary supply is important, and the supply chain is important. All these things need to work together. The primary financial function of a central government is to be sure the monetary system is sound and there is adequate money to grease the wheels of the economic system. Federal stimulus to deal with any demand shock needs to be quick and direct. This happened in 2020, but it did not happen during the Great Depression. Remember, it was World War II that put an end to the Depression, thanks to wages and salaries paid to millions of citizens who went to work in the military and defense plants. This resurrected the economy. This unintended but necessary stimulus was large and quick, and the Depression ended. Many thought the US would go back into depression after the war ended, but this was not to be the case. The US emerged from the Great Depression and the war as the undisputed world economic and military power.

This has been an expensive learning process. We learned during the Great Depression we should never allow our banks to fail. This learning helped us survive the financial crisis of 2008–09 as the Federal Reserve, with help from Congress and the president, kept our financial system floating.

We learned from the 1970s it is essential to not let inflation get a serious foothold in the economy. It must be dealt with earlier and not later. The pain is just too great. I have often thought the 1981–82 recession was the Great Recession, not the one in 2008–09. The 2008–09 recession was more dangerous, but not more severe.

We learned in 2020 and 2021 that you must not shut down a

national or state economy. It was a colossal mistake. Economies must continue to produce, or everything falls apart. Putting it back together again is expensive and lengthy. It is all too easy to panic, and we did.

The two most influential economists of the twentieth and twenty-first centuries have been John Maynard Keynes and Milton Friedman. Their influence is felt today in the United States and indeed, across the world. A study of their writings is essential to a full understanding of how the economic world works. We have learned much, but sometimes our leaders seem to forget, and then we repeat the same lessons. We need to remind them of our economic history.

CHAPTER 6

THE SOCIALISM ATTRACTION

The rise of big government, particularly beginning in the twentieth century, provided a springboard for a level of official intrusion into the lives of citizens never before possible. Modern systems of communication and information flow made even the smallest items of a person's life available for scrutiny. The cyber-sphere knows more about us than we know about ourselves. It is aware of what we purchase, what movies we like, what books we read, what our political persuasion is, what our hobbies are, and what our medical concerns include. In addition, it provides a great deal of financial information about our activities.

The income tax itself would have been exceedingly difficult to administer in earlier times, when information concerning income was unavailable for most economic activities. The whole system and infrastructure of withholding income taxes from paychecks was not possible prior to the development of the industrial age and the growth of company staffs and government information-gathering systems. The first income tax was put in effect during the Civil War, but the tax was neither effective nor popular.[1] Congress repealed the tax law in 1871. However, the Sixteenth Amendment to the Constitution authorized a US income tax and was ratified in 1913. By that time, the tax collection process was much more effective, and income taxes began to comprise a significant percentage of the federal budget. It has remained so ever since. Many states followed suit and adopted a state income tax to augment their treasuries. Prior to 1913, not reporting your income was not a criminal activity.

The Sixteenth Amendment to the Constitution reads as follows:

> The Congress shall have the power to levy and collect taxes on incomes, from whatever source derived, without apportionment among the several states, and without regard to any census or enumeration.[2]

Well, talk about giving a blank check to Uncle Sam! Notice the language placed no limit on the income tax. The Sixteenth Amendment left the states out and instituted a dump truck convoy of tax money directly to Washington that has continued ever since.

For socialism to thrive and flourish, it needs *lots* of cash. We frequently hear the admonition: "Follow the money." This is certainly true when attempting to solve a money crime, and it is also true when examining government power and influence. In this case, we can just follow the money pipeline straight to Washington, DC.

> The problem with socialism is that eventually you run out of other people's money.[3] (Margaret Thatcher)

In a democracy, money can buy obedience to whatever the central government wants to do. It simply tells the recipient of the benefits to do what they are told, or the money stops. It is economic coercion, but, unfortunately, it is very effective, and it generally flies under the radar. Additionally, money can result in the setting up of vast agencies and departments that, by their nature, gobble cash and gush forth new rules and regulations every day.

Socialism creeps up on a capitalist democracy much like the proverbial frog being boiled slowly in a pot of water. The frog fails to realize that circumstances are changing—until it is too late. It can happen to a free-enterprise, free-market society in much the same way. The basic direction is a slow but steady sacrifice of freedom in exchange for security. Want a government retirement? Give up your decision-making power over your own retirement. Want government healthcare? Sacrifice your ability to control your own healthcare decisions. The list continues. And by the way, send more money to the powers that be.

> If freedom is to survive and prosper, it will require the sacrifice, the effort, and the thoughtful attention of every citizen.[4] (John F. Kennedy)

In my opinion, President Kennedy was not only an advocate for freedom, he was a supply-sider. His proposal in 1963 to cut both personal and corporate taxes was designed to promote economic growth. This measure was passed after his death in 1964 and would not be replicated again until the Reagan tax cuts of the 1980s.

Few of us would opt for communism or fascism, but we seem comfortable with a system that is moving slowly in that direction. Governments want more revenue, and they offer grand-sounding enticements and a long list of goodies to citizens—in exchange for their freedoms. We hear about equity and equality, fair shares, saving the environment, taxing the rich, peace in our time, free this-and-that, and the list goes on and on. The glaring problem is that government's track record on all of these issues is quite disappointing. Yet we remain tempted to travel down a road which has been traveled many times before with little success and great cost.

Regarding fairness, economist Dr. Thomas Sowell summed it up well when he asserted: "Some people seem to think that, if life is not fair, then the answer is to turn more of the nation's resources over to politicians—who will, of course, then spend these resources in ways that increase the politicians' chances of getting reelected."[5]

There is no question that life is unfair. It is a fact, and we see it everywhere. Some people are taller than others, some are more attractive, some have more athletic ability, some are born to prosperous parents, some live in a better economic and social environment. The list is endless. The larger question: can *government* do anything about this unfairness? The obvious follow-up question is: who is going to determine what is fair and what is not fair? Advocates of socialism really seem to believe government can bring about fairness and equity for its citizens. The problem here is that central governments, throughout human history, have never been able to even come close to achieving these goals.

The Declaration of Independence is clear about equality:

> We hold these truths to be self-evident, that all men are created equal, that they are endowed by their Creator with certain unalienable rights, that among these are Life, Liberty, and the pursuit of happiness.

The Declaration directly addresses "Life, Liberty, and the pursuit of happiness." Life and liberty are rights, but happiness is not. Only the *pursuit* of happiness is a right. A nation that strives to give every citizen the opportunity to succeed will be successful. Much can be done to help those who start out with some hindrances. One is a free K-12 education to allow the young to prepare themselves for the future. However, some will take full advantage of this opportunity, and some will not. Another is to guarantee that the education provided is quality, which has been frequently not the case.

A strong effort must be made to ensure that opportunities are provided for all. This is essential. Discrimination limits the success of the individual, and it also limits the success of a nation. If every citizen is given the opportunity to function at their highest level, the total level of national production will be higher than otherwise, and the country will be more prosperous. It is in the best interest of a nation for every person to be employed efficiently and productively.

The key to prosperity is *production*. Capitalism gives workers the opportunity to participate in the production of goods and services and to benefit personally. In the private sector, wages and salaries depend on the productivity of workers. A low-productivity worker can hardly expect a high salary, and yet a high-productivity worker will certainly expect a high salary, or they will leave for greener pastures. It is in the best interest of the business to match the productivity with the compensation. This is fair. It is not taking advantage of anyone. Many workers are capable of producing at a higher level, and the lure of a higher salary might cause them to strive even harder. A higher level of effort, additional certification, training, or other educational attainment might be just what is needed. Perhaps a new opportunity with a different employer may also be appropriate. Productive employees generally have a great many options.

America is a land of opportunity. The very fact that we have a free-market economy provides the potential for success. When you look at entrepreneurship, America leads the way. Citizens have complete job mobility. They can quit one job and move to another. They can move completely across the country in search of a job. Opportunity is everywhere and knocks on the door of the productive almost every day.

Caveats exist. We must show up to work. We must work hard. We can't steal from our employer. We can't be rude to our customers. We must do our job. For some employees, this is too much to ask. Well, if that is the case, life is going to be tough, and others are going to move ahead, be more successful, and make more money.

According to King Solomon: "there is nothing new under the sun."[6] Top-down government control has been tried before. In fact, the American colonists revolted against British authorities to escape control and create a nation and a government that valued *freedom*. They risked life, fortune, and family to break away from tyranny and coercion to live a life of self-determination and freedom.

Governments tend to overpromise and underachieve. In the

process, they damage the productive capacity of the economy. Remember, we are turning over increased decision-making power and the cash needed to enforce these decisions to the world's largest monopolist, Uncle Sam. The proposed budget for the US federal government for fiscal year 2023 was $6.2 trillion, three times the size of the entire economy of Russia.[7] Good government is good, but when government gets too big, too bloated, too cumbersome, and too expensive—then not so much. In 2021, American entrepreneur Elon Musk stated: "Eventually they run out of other people's money, and then they come for you."[8] This was his version of Margaret Thatcher's earlier statement on socialism.

Musk's statement was in response to large tax increases being promoted by the Biden administration. He referred primarily to a proposed wealth tax on unrealized capital gains. In other words, you have not sold the property (or securities or stock) yet, but the government will tax it anyway. Musk followed up with this statement, "My plan is to use the money to get humanity to Mars and preserve the light of consciousness."[9] Mr. Musk was defending the idea that his money is his money because he earned it and would like to decide how to spend it himself.

This reminds me of the Tom Cruise movie *Minority Report*. The plot involves the police use of a psychic process to arrest and convict individuals for crimes they are going to commit in the future. This is pretty close to the idea of taxing American citizens on the value of their property now. As we well know, property and investment values come and go. It also follows that even if you have something of value, you may not have the cash to pay the tax. It's a far-out idea that is being presented as sensible taxation policy.

Socialism is a type of the Pied Piper of Hamlin, who played mystically enchanting music and led the children astray. However, when we arrive at our new destination, we are likely to exclaim: what were we thinking?

You can generally recognize a socialist because

- They like to talk about redistributing income and wealth.
- They rarely talk about creating income and wealth.
- They love taxes and government programs.
- They love government mandates.

Many may remember John F. Kennedy's statement in 1963: "A rising tide raises all boats."[10] President Kennedy was the first president to apply supply-side economics principles to a modern economy. In 1963 he proposed tax cuts aimed at stimulating economic growth by cutting the top personal tax rate from 90 percent to 70 percent.[11] President Reagan followed this same path in the 1980s, cutting the top bracket from 70 percent to 50 percent and then to 28 percent.[12] The record-setting economic growth that followed is undeniably impressive.

Kennedy knew if economic growth was stimulated, the nation's citizens would benefit economically. This is not a socialist mindset. The socialist mindset is redistribution. Redistribution generally leads to slower economic growth. The incentives for production are reduced for both those who lose income and wealth and for those on the receiving end of the process.

An American businessman, author, and investor made an interesting comment about the processes of non-capitalistic economic systems.

> Capitalism and competition create wealth; other systems slop existing wealth around.[13] (Andy Kessler)

Socialism is attractive because of the charm of lofty promises and because it is usually sold on the basis that *someone else* will pay. Promises are easy to make but tougher to keep. On the contrary, capitalism is not built on promises. It is built on personal responsibility, hard work, sacrifice for personal goals, and innovative thinking. Yes, the results can be uneven. The individual who strives to get a good education, expands their training, performs exceptional work, and displays honesty and reliability is likely to flourish and thrive. The individual who does none of these things is unlikely to prosper. Some believe that different results for different people is unfair. However, remember, fairness is in the eye of the beholder. I doubt hardworking citizens would deem it fair if we took the fruit of their labor away and gave it to those who are capable but unwilling to be productive. I also doubt high-achieving college students would want their A's taken away and redistributed to the seldom-attenders and regular no-shows.

In 1964, President Lyndon Johnson announced his "Great Society" vision during a commencement speech at the University of Michigan.[14] Designed and articulated to end poverty, reduce crime, improve the environment, end inequality, and expand healthcare, it was an ambitious package of programs. It vastly expanded the role of government in the economy (similar to many of the Great Depression programs of the 1930s). The basic elements of Johnson's Great Society included the following:

- War on Poverty
- Medicare and Medicaid
- Project Head Start
- Urban Renewal
- National Endowment for the Humanities
- Water Quality Act

The goals of the "Great Society" are laudatory. However, the basic question remains: To what extent can government accomplish all of this, and how much freedom will be lost in the process? Remember, if the benefits come from government, then the rules will come from government. I doubt you will find anyone in America who believes we do not *still* have inequality, poverty, crime, injustice, environmental issues, and healthcare challenges. In fact, the Biden administration, in 2021, proposed massive new programs to deal with the precise issues that Johnson's Great Society aimed to eradicate, accompanied by hefty new tax increases to pay for it all. Undoubtedly, some future administration will also propose new programs and hefty taxes to deal with the very same issues. And on it goes. Two constants remain: the issues remain the issues, and the central government grows larger, larger, and larger.

> Government is not the solution to our problem; government is the problem …. Government does not solve problems; it subsidizes them. Government's view of the economy could be summed up in a few short phrases: If it moves, tax it. If it keeps moving, regulate it. If it stops moving, subsidize it. The problem is not that the government taxes too little, the problem is that government spends too much.[15] (Ronald Reagan)

In a capitalistic system, the best thing you can do for an individual is help them get a good education or quality training that empowers and equips them to do for themselves. In this way, not only is the individual benefited, but a stronger and more prosperous nation will result. Americans have generous hearts and genuinely want to help those who cannot fend for themselves. There are expansive government programs and many private charities that provide help and assistance with these efforts. But when we subsidize nonwork for the potentially productive, we waste a valuable human resource that could be enhancing their own personal good as well as the national good.

The key here is to get the poor into the production process. Presently, the United States has a massive public assistance program that rewards non-production. Why not change it to reward production? As citizens produce, they should benefit. The more productive they become, the more they should benefit. As poor and low-income citizens become more productive, they simultaneously reduce inequalities of income. If an individual is locked in a system that rewards non-production, then the status quo continues. The inequality also continues, sponsored by government itself. It is only as people move off the bottom rung of the economic ladder that income inequality can effectively be reduced. If they are incentivized to stay where they are, then the problem just continues in a never-ending cycle.

Socialism remains attractive because of all the promises. The Bolsheviks made a lot of promises leading up to and through the Russian Revolution. But it did not work out so well for the revolutionaries. Remember those seventy-four years of destruction!

In 1959, Fidel Castro made promises about good times to come. It also did not happen, and it will never happen under a communist system. The same thing happened in China when Mao Zedong won the communist revolution in 1949 and became the founder of the People's Republic of China. It was a republic in name only and ushered in brutality and oppression. Ironically, communist governments always seem to have high-sounding names. Remember the USSR, the Union of Soviet Socialist Republics? How about the Democratic People's Republic of Korea in North Korea for the name of a country with a despotic ruler?

It was only in the late 1970s, after the death of Mao Zedong, that Chinese leaders experimented with injecting some freedom of enterprise and private property rights into their economy. As indicated by the comments of my colleague Dr. Zhao (see chapter 3), who grew up during this period, a little economic freedom can energize a backward economic system. But these policies can only be allowed to go so far, because freedom is infectious. Indeed, there are current indications that the PRC is tightening down on some of the economic freedoms that have naturally developed in the Chinese economy, as those freedoms are now considered to be a threat to the leader's power.

Autocratic socialism can work but only with a lot of brutality and force. Democratic socialism can work, but it takes a lot of coercion and control. Neither of the systems sounds particularly attractive to me. The promises are attractive. The results are not.

CHAPTER 7

IN SEARCH OF UTOPIA

This side of heaven, utopia does not and will never exist in reality. However, it does exist in the minds of those who would like to use coercive power to achieve what they envision. The term "utopia" comes from Sir Thomas More's book with the same title written in 1516.[1] More's *Utopia* is a fictional island community where near-perfect conditions exist within the social, political, and legal spheres. The Oxford Languages Dictionary defines utopia as "an imagined place or state of things in which everything is perfect."[2] Ironically, the word originates from the Greek "ou" and "topos," meaning "no place."[3]

It will never happen, but this does not dissuade advocates of the concept who labor diligently to bring it about. They work passionately to usher in this supposed perfect place and continue to promote the role of central government in creating it. Additionally, they strive mightily to ensure that they, along with like-minded associates, will be in control of that government. Many of these advocates seem very flexible with regard to the methods used to achieve this control.

It is tempting for socialism enthusiasts to promote the idea that socialism improves on capitalism but does not incorporate the negatives of communism or fascism. Proponents frequently tell us that capitalism has flaws and only socialism can remedy the situation. But they ignore the fact that socialism has much *worse* flaws. In the search for perfection, socialism advocates lead the nation away from what works very well toward a system that does *not* work very well. In the process, society moves gradually in the direction of autocratic socialism (communism/fascism), and the individual citizen loses more and more freedom.

Advocates of socialism promote two primary themes to move a nation in their direction. The first theme (which we will talk about more in chapter 13) involves a focus on winners and losers.

SOCIALISM – PRINCIPLE ONE

> Capitalism picks winners and losers, and this is inherently unfair. Only government policy can level the playing field to ensure there are no losers and that the winners do not win too much.

In capitalism, the productive are rewarded and the non-productive are not rewarded. That is just the way it is. My mother constantly quoted the saying, "Early to bed and early to rise makes a man healthy, wealthy, and wise." She would then follow up with "The early bird gets the worm." This was part of my upbringing that pounded in the point there is no free lunch out there, and if you want to prosper, you must get with it. The power of this process is that citizens need to be motivated to be productive. It is a reward system based on *production*. Because it encourages production, capitalism consistently creates the most total economic activity together with a higher standard of living for its citizens when compared to other systems.

Remember, compare the real with the real. Do not compare the real with the imagined. Do not compare the real with someone's vision of utopia. Compare the real with the real. Productivity leads to prosperity.

American journalist and economic commentator Henry Hazlitt

made the following insightful comment about production and poverty:

> The real problem of poverty is not a problem of "distribution" but of production. The poor are not poor because something is being withheld from them but because, for whatever reason, they are not producing enough. The only permanent way to cure their poverty is to increase their earning power.[4] (Henry Hazlitt)

This powerful statement is generally ignored by those who support massive government programs to address poverty. Their typical solution is to redistribute *existing* income and wealth from the productive to the non- or less-productive. They have no plan to create *additional* income and wealth. This process rewards non-production, which is exactly what should not be rewarded. The key to prosperity is production. Citizens must *not* be locked in a government-supported assistance system where production is not rewarded and is even penalized.

Prior to becoming our sixteenth president, Abraham Lincoln penned these words about production:

> Inasmuch as most good things are produced by labor, it follows that all such things of right belong to those whose labor has produced them. But it has so happened, in all ages of the world, that some have labored, and others have without labor enjoyed a large proportion of the fruits. This is wrong, and should not continue. To secure to each laborer the whole product of his labor, or as nearly as possible, is a worthy subject of any good government.[5]

We need programs that reward production and also preparation for production. The more our population produces, the higher the standard of living will be for everyone. Citizens who are incentivized not to produce harm total national output.

Production must be the key mindset of our population. It needs to be emphasized at all levels of education. If this is the case, young people will instinctively know what they must do to be successful. Preparation is the cornerstone. Hard work and diligence are the follow-ups. The idea that we can just tax the rich and redistribute their wealth is a bankrupt idea. If it worked, it would have worked somewhere in the world by now.

A friend of mine, at twelve years of age and through an assortment of odd jobs, accumulated a savings account of $3,200 back in the 1960s. By the time he graduated from a local university, he had $40,000 in the bank that he used to purchase a local grocery store. Years later when he retired, he had accumulated eight stores. This is the power of capitalism. Not only did my friend do good for himself, but by providing grocery services throughout his area, he provided a service, met needs in the market, and employed hundreds of citizens.

Regardless, the socialist will generally state it is not fair for the entrepreneur to prosper while some others do not. The redistribution of income is prominent in their discussions. They focus on income taxes, inheritance taxes, and wealth taxes as powerful tools for accomplishing the goal of redistribution. It all sounds so good, but the social and economic impact is damaging.

SOCIALISM – PRINCIPLE TWO

> Many inequities exist in society. Only government has the ability to end discrimination, lack of opportunity, ageism, sexism, etc. The costs of these efforts are worth the money and coercion necessary to deal with these issues.

The problem? We can never know if or when all of these wonderful utopian goals are actually accomplished. In the meantime, big central government just keeps chugging along, gobbling incomes and guzzling freedom in a continuous never-ending motion. Life cannot be perfect. By its nature, it is challenging, and people are far from perfect. A government attempting to implement perfection accomplishes nothing but disappointment and a growing dissatisfaction with government itself. To be sensible and practical, we must remember to compare the real with the real.

For those who press for utopia, I pose a question. From all of history, where does this utopia exist, or where has it ever existed? The answer is, "nowhere and never." Socialist nations have not achieved utopia, although their citizens have surrendered significant amounts of liberty and treasure in the name of achieving it. The nations employing capitalism come the closest, but they will never achieve it either. Utopia exists only in the minds of those who would use power and coercion to achieve it. The very fact that power and coercion will be used is proof that it will be no utopia. Again, *compare the real with the real.* Utopia is not real, and it will never be on this earth. Regrettably, that fact does not prevent people from searching for it and damaging their own economies and societies in the quest to implement it.

> There is no such thing as "safe" socialism. If it's safe, it's not socialism. And if it's socialism, it's not safe. The signposts of socialism point downhill to less freedom, less prosperity, downhill to more muddle, more failure. If we follow them to their destination, they will lead this nation into bankruptcy.[6] (Margaret Thatcher)

People make better decisions about what they need than do governments. This frustrates the socialists, because we do not behave as they would like us to behave. We do different things. We like different things. We are interested in creative ideas. Beyond military service, the marching band, or synchronized swimming, we do not find it attractive to march in lockstep. After all, that is what freedom is all about. As long as we live within the rule of law and do no harm to our neighbor, we want to be left alone. Let "we the people" live our own lives. Let us be free to determine our own version of utopia. Based on our current population, this philosophy would result in 331 million versions of the pursuit of happiness, not just one.

As Alan Keyes, Assistant Secretary of State in the 1980s, stated,

> What is self-government about, after all? What is this society about? They certainly are not about producing a utopia through the instrument of the state. Even if government could produce all that it promises, we would not want those results on the terms they are offered. They are terms that require that we surrender a good that is more important than good results: our freedom to make choices.[7] (Alan Keyes)

> Socialism in general has a record of failure so blatant that only an intellectual could ignore or evade it.[8] (Thomas Sowell)

The quest for utopia continues. Advocates for the dream will not be deterred. Each has a different vision of utopia, but nearly all want to use coercive power to make it happen. Socialism is attractive because all of the promises are attractive. The promises are attractive because they are so easy to make. Let's keep government out of the utopia business.

CHAPTER 8

THE CORONAVIRUS AND LOCKDOWN DISASTER

THE YEAR OF OUR LORD 2020 STARTED OUT AS A PROSPEROUS AND hopeful year with virtually all economic indicators in the "Doing Great" zone. In February, the unemployment rate was 3.5 percent, the rate of inflation was in the 2 percent range, interest rates were low, and the economy was growing at a healthy rate.[1] The consumer confidence index was high, and everything pointed to good times ahead.

Everything changed in January and February. The novel coronavirus hit the United States and the world, and on March 13 President Donald Trump declared a national emergency.[2] This emergency was extended and finally ended on April 30. Immediately the states began various levels and degrees of state shutdowns. In many states, citizens were simply told to stay home. The result? A dramatic quarterly decline in the national real GDP, which amounted to a 32.9 percent negative rate in the second quarter.[3] Although the national emergency was lifted in April, many state governors and mayors continued their lockdowns. The resulting economic devastation was widespread. Did we not think this would happen if we simply *stopped producing*?

The national unemployment rate reached 14.7 percent in April, and it appeared the US was headed for a second Great Depression.[4] You cannot simply pull a switch and shut down a nation's economy without severe economic and social repercussions. But we did it anyway. We did not fully consider the consequences. We panicked, and we have paid the consequences.

Flashback to the Great Depression in the 1930s. As a result of the bank failures discussed earlier in chapters 4 and 5, the unemployment rate reached 25 percent, and the GDP of the nation declined by nearly 50 percent (29 percent, adjusted for inflation).[5] Instead of the usual inflation, the nation experienced deflation. Prices actually went down. This situation resulted from a lack of demand to purchase goods and services available at the existing prices. It wasn't a supply shock, it was a demand shock. Everything was suddenly at fire-sale prices. Banks failed by the thousands, depositors lost their funds, and the economy spiraled down. *There was simply no money.* The barter system returned as people started selling and swapping their worldly possessions just to stay alive, provide for their next meal, put a roof over their heads, and perhaps keep the farm. The Depression ebbed and flowed during the 1930s but did not really end until the outbreak of World War II.

In the spring of 2020, when the US declared a national emergency and the lockdowns began, the nation headed for a repeat at breakneck pace. Something had to be done and be done quickly. That something was the CARES Act. President Trump signed the Coronavirus Aid, Relief and Economic Security Act into law on March 27, 2020.[6] This bipartisan legislation was a $2.2 trillion effort to prevent the economic tailspin from continuing. The CARES Act was actually the third relief bill signed into law. The first $8.3 billion bill (March 6, 2020) promoted coronavirus vaccine research and development, and the second (March 18, 2020) included $104 billion for sick leave and unemployment benefits.[7]

What is remarkable is that Congress and the president acted so quickly in reaction to the impact of the virus and the shutdowns. It demonstrates that, when the chips are down, government can respond. However, this all happened after the economic devastation caused by the national emergency and actual state and city shutdowns. This is yet another example of government creating a problem and then following up with programs to save us from the problem it created. It is worth noting that a number of states did not shut down their economies and fared well during the pandemic. This is particularly the case when the stimulus money came rolling in, as their economies had not suffered very much economically to start with.

The CARES Act dump-trucked trillions of dollars on the economy in short order. This should have been done in response to the Great Depression in the 1930s, but it was not. In 2020, the federal government and the Federal Reserve System acted appropriately and promptly. The federal government provided the fiscal stimulus through big spending, and the Federal Reserve System kept the financial system sound and the money flowing. Much of this stimulus included direct payments to citizens. This put cash in the hands of the public quickly and eased the pain of the shutdowns. This is classic "helicopter money."

The Federal Reserve ensured that the massive government borrowing for the coronavirus response was accommodated. The Fed financed the Treasury borrowing, and the money flowed. The US actually financed most of its own borrowing, and the bond account of the Federal Reserve expanded rapidly. We were borrowing from ourselves, and it is a neat trick as long as inflation remains under control. However, after the shutdowns took effect, these actions were necessary and appropriate, and the Fed had the capacity to do it. Of course, all of this would not have been necessary with a more reasoned approach to the virus outbreak in the first place.

Some categories of spending in the CARES Act included the following:[8]

$1,200	Direct Stimulus Payments	To every taxpayer
$500	Child Credit	Per child
$600	Unemployment Payments	In addition to the amount the state paid

$350B	Small Business	Closure & layoff prevention
$500B	Large Business	Loans
$140B	Hospitals & Healthcare	
$150B	State & Local Governments	

As a result of all this spending and in conjunction with the lifting of the national emergency, the economy began its recovery in the third quarter of 2020. The real GDP expanded by 33.1 percent in the third quarter.[9] The lockdown cratered the economy in the second quarter, but the CARES Act resurrected it in the third. Looking at these results, it tells us the shocking cost of a national lockdown. The cost started out above $2.2 trillion dollars but ended up being a lot more than that. But the US economy was saved.

The fiscal year 2020 US budget deficit came in at $3.1 trillion for the fiscal year ending September 30, which was $2 trillion over the original forecast.[10] President Trump signed another relief bill on December 27, 2020 that amounted to $908 billion in additional spending.[11] At the time, I referred to this bill as "recession insurance" to prevent the possibility of a slide back into a recession during early 2021.

The December stimulus bill included (but was not limited to) the following categories of spending:[12]

$600	Direct Stimulus Payment
$300/week	Additional Unemployment Payments
$232B	Small Business
$58B	Vaccine Program
$45B	Transportation
$25B	Rental Assistance
$82B	Schools & Colleges

In early 2021, the new Biden administration wanted to get in on the action and passed a strictly partisan $1.9 trillion bill with many of the same types of stimulus payments included in the original CARES Act.[13] I believed this stimulus bill represented a significant level of overkill. But it certainly juiced economic growth. The current dollar rate of GDP growth reached 6.4 percent for the first quarter of 2021, 6.6 percent in the second, 7.8 percent in the third quarter, and 7.0 percent in the fourth. However, the real rate of GDP growth (after adjustment for inflation) was only 2.0 percent in the third and 2.3 percent in the fourth quarter. It is a reminder that current dollar economic growth can occur simply due to an increase in the general level of prices, which it did.

The rate of inflation for the entire year of 2021 was 6.5 percent and heralded the more serious inflation problems to be experienced in 2022.[14] This inflation was a result of strong demand for goods and services and widespread labor and product shortages. The December 2020 stimulus and the March 2021 stimulus continued to provide cash incentives for workers to stay home; at the same time, the economy was taking off, and the demand for workers was high. The extra unemployment benefits finally ended in September 2021.

What I do know is *we cannot do this again*. The economic destruction is too great.

The virus proved a serious problem for older citizens, particularly those with preexisting conditions. For the rest of the population, the risk of death turned out to be low. The following chart displays survival rates for various age groups as tabulated by the Centers for Disease Control and Prevention:[15]

Age Group	Survival Rate
0-19	99.99%
20-49	99.98%
50-69	99.5%
70+	94.6%

As you can see, the risk has been concentrated primarily in the older age groups. The nineteen and younger age group was at little risk. The fact that many K-12 schools remained closed for lengthy periods seems pointlessly destructive to the social, developmental, and educational lives of students. Studies have documented the educational damage to K-12 students, and the results were unsurprisingly negative.[16] For a great many students, it was a lost year of education, though the students themselves were at little risk of serious illness.

It also became quickly clear early in the pandemic that those citizens in the normal working-age groups were also in a low-risk category. The economy could have remained open with only a small risk to the general population. Many governors did exactly that, and their states and citizens benefited enormously compared to the lockdown states. The unemployment rates in open states were notably lower during the pandemic as the wheels of business and industry kept turning. Ironically, lockdown states did *not* perform better regarding virus statistics.

In December 2020, as a guest on Roby Brock's *Talk Business and Politics* television show in Little Rock, Arkansas, I told Roby I believed March 2021 would be the beginning of a return to normal for the nation.[17] Why did I believe that? I am not a medical professional. I am an economist, but economists love numbers. Let me explain how I arrived at my prediction.

By the conclusion of March 2021, approximately 100 million Americans were projected to have received the vaccine for the existing strain. At that point, approximately 30 million citizens were documented to have already had the virus. Some medical experts believed another 2 or 3 times as many might have actually had the virus but were never tested. An additional 110 million Americans aged 24 or younger were at virtually no risk from the virus. There was certainly some double-counting here, but what we had was the fact that perhaps 250 million citizens would not be at much risk.

Virtually every person over 65 who wanted the vaccine had access to it by March 2021.

The projection turned out to be accurate, as people began bursting out in March 2021 and returning to some semblance of normal life. People began to travel, eat out, socialize, shop in stores, attend sporting events, and engage in a great variety of recreational activities. In spite of a spike in cases in the fall of 2021 due to the Delta variant, people continued to return to normalcy as indicated by the crowds at football games and other events across the country. People were ready to move on and get back to normal, and the majority of them exercised thoughtful, commonsense health and safety measures of their own choosing. It turned out the spike in the fall may have had a lot to do with vaccine efficacy diminishing after five or six months.

It is hindsight, but we should have avoided the shutdowns. It was too draconian, and the nation is paying the price. Here in Arkansas, Governor Hutchinson asked citizens to limit certain activities but otherwise let them use their own common sense and good judgment. The economic benefits of this approach proved dramatic, with Arkansas unemployment reaching pre-pandemic levels long before lockdown states saw anywhere near that level of success.

This approach worked in other states as well. It is important to remember that states don't have a Federal Reserve to lend them money at the drop of a hat. They must make their budgets balance, which in turn means they must keep economic reality in mind and keep the doors open.

As a nation, we learned a lot about a pandemic, and we also learned how much a draconian response to a pandemic can cost. This *cannot* be future policy when dealing with a similar emergency, pandemic or otherwise. If we break the federal government and wreck the economy, I doubt there is anyone out there who will bail us out. We must be more cautious about limiting economic activity in the future. As Elon Musk said, "If you don't make stuff, there's no stuff."[18]

If people don't go to work, there is no stuff.

CHAPTER 9

THE ECONOMIC DEATH WISH

THE 2020 CORONAVIRUS PANDEMIC CREATED SOME CHALLENGING results from an economic standpoint because of the nature of the virus and the nature of the response. Many of our nation's governors and mayors displayed an almost total misunderstanding of the basic principles of economics and data analysis.

The United States operates under the principle of federalism. The Encyclopedia Britannica refers to federalism as a "mode of political organization that unites separate states or other polities within an overarching political system in a way that allows each to maintain its own integrity."[1] There are areas of national government power, areas of state government power, and areas of overlapping government power.

The bottom line is the federal government was not intended as the be-all and end-all. The writers of the Constitution had had enough of that with the British parliament and King George III. The American states were to possess sovereignty and power, and the founders believed this was a good thing. It was. And it is.

Federalism allows states to be different and for each to pursue policies it believes are best for its citizens. This is a vast country with striking differences in geography and population. What works for one state may not work for another. Therefore, in many areas, policies need to be different from state to state. *This is good for freedom.* What one state can afford, another may not. What one state wants, another may not. State policies can be dramatically distinct and richly diverse, making the United States the wonderfully creative nation it is.

During the pandemic, we saw this work out in a real-life example of federalism. We saw the world's financial capital in New York City shut down while other cities continued to function. We saw citizens of some states told to stay home, while citizens of other states moved about with few limitations. In effect, there were national pandemic guidelines and fifty individual state sets of guidelines. You might think a national set of guidelines would have been better. But *which* set? The set that produced economic destruction and unemployment at nosebleed levels, or the set that allowed most business and industry activities to proceed—resulting in much lower unemployment levels because citizens got to keep their jobs?

Some of the states got it right, and some got it wrong. How could those who got it wrong be so wrong and for so long? Why did these governors persist in state lockdowns long after the national emergency was over? Did they enjoy exercising power, or were they just utterly unaware of the economic destruction their policies would generate?

If lockdowns work, why don't they work?

Lockdown governors need to be tremendously thankful that the federal government had some powder dry and the capacity to unload billions of dollars of relief to each of the fifty states. Otherwise, we would have witnessed massive state and city financial problems, and their citizens would have suffered for it. States with more sensible policies prospered, and many actually saw their state revenues increase—for some, dramatically.

Decisions have consequences. Government actions have consequences. Policies have consequences. Based on what many people witnessed and experienced during the pandemic, some of our states appeared to have had an economic death wish. They apparently thought the principles of capitalism and economics simply did not apply to them. High tax rates and layers of regulations had already hobbled some of our most prosperous states, even before the pandemic. Add to this an inhospitable economic climate, and many people bailed from these states in search of more commonsense environments. Between April 2020 and July 2021, California's population declined by 300,387, a 0.8 percent decline.[2] This was very unusual for a state used to population growth. Between 2007 and 2016 more than 1,000,000 citizens left for other states, with Texas, Arizona, and Nevada being the most popular go-to destinations.[3]

While some states look at tax increases to fund expanding government programs, others look at creating a more citizen and business tax-friendly environment. Many have lowered, or are in the process of lowering, income tax rates and have worked to attract retirees with tax reduction incentives. Nine states have no state income taxes on wage and salary income: Alaska, Florida, Nevada, New Hampshire, South Dakota, Tennessee, Texas, Washington, and Wyoming.[4]

The Tax Foundation ranked California 48th in the nation based on their State Business Climate Index for 2022. Implications of the impact of all this seem supported by the move of Tesla to Texas, accompanied by Charles Schwab, Oracle, and Hewlett Packard. Texas ranks 14th in the same listing with Florida 4th and Nevada 7th.[5]

Over the years, I taught my students the definition of economics as "a study of the allocation of scarce resources for the maximum satisfaction of human wants." Resources are limited, but our wants are unlimited. What is needed is an economic system that can allocate resources efficiently. Capitalism, with all its warts and imperfections (because we have warts and imperfections), *is* that system. During all the history of humankind, no better system has ever been discovered. And believe you me, many have been tried.

Why are the leaders in some of our most prosperous states pursuing policies that impede economic activity and raise the cost of nearly everything? Increasing taxes and regulations has consequences. Too many government leaders think they can vastly expand the role of government and that private individuals and businesses will just keep doing what they normally do. But this is not the case. *Behavior will change.* For every change in policy, there is a human reaction. Reactions result in changes in behavior. And these behavioral changes have consequences.

Changes in taxes and regulations will produce changes in behavior.

In California, Governor Newsom signed a piece of legislation that will undoubtedly produce unintended consequences. The act is high-minded, as it is aimed at improving the environment. It requires the state's Air Resources Board to effectively eliminate the sale of new gas-powered, small, off-road engines in the state by 2024 (or by whenever the Board determines feasible).[6]

The bill appeared to be aimed at such machines as chainsaws, Weed eaters, lawnmowers, generators, and other fossil-fueled equipment. I have two chainsaws. One is gasoline-powered, and the other is battery-driven. They are both great pieces of equipment with a particular application. If I have a quick light job, the battery-powered saw will do. If it is a bigger job, perhaps one that will last all day, the gasoline-powered saw is what I need. The battery-powered saw is new and the first one I have ever owned. I like it. But it does not replace my gas saw; it complements it.

Several things would happen if my state (unlikely) would issue such an edict. The first is that I, and others, would likely make an extra effort to keep the old saw running. I have several older saws that have seen better days, but I would probably want to get them running as a backup. The second is that I would probably drive over the state line if I needed to buy a new gas-powered saw. Notice that this initiative would change my economic decision-making. As I mentioned earlier, this law would *change my behavior*. Why should government interfere with normal commerce? The move to battery power will happen naturally when it is time, and it is certainly occurring as we speak. The move from buggy whips to gas throttles in the early 1900s was not achieved as a result of a government mandate. Citizens can make these decisions through the marketplace when it makes economic sense, and the government's efforts can be directed toward fixing the potholes.

On January 1, 2023, in Seattle, Washington, the minimum wage increased to $18.69 per hour. This is an annual wage of $38,875.[7] The employer pays Social Security taxes and unemployment taxes on top of this total. This means the least-skilled worker in a particular job costs the employer more than $38,875 each year. You can see this amounts to a serious hindrance for a low-skilled and or young employee to get a job. It is also a huge incentive for employers to add more capital and technology to their business model to reduce their reliance on lower-skilled workers. This is a prime example of a government rule designed to help people that ends up hurting those who need the most help. The high-skilled worker has nothing to fear from the minimum wage.

California Assembly Bill AB5, which went into effect January 1, 2020, makes it more difficult for an individual to be categorized as an independent contractor in the state. The law was primarily aimed at Uber, Lyft, and other independent contractors.[8] However, it is also affecting independent truck drivers. If a contractor does not meet the ABC test, then they must be categorized as employees. The problem is that moving contractors to employee status can be quite expensive, and many contractors like the independence they enjoy. Many of us have ridden with Uber or Lyft. In my discussions with drivers, I have discovered that many of them have full-time jobs elsewhere and like to make extra income driving when they have time. This is a perfect independent contractor situation. These types of state restrictions increase costs and limit opportunities for individuals to work independently. States applying these types of restrictions will undoubtedly find they are less attractive to individuals and companies trying to make a profit and keep their economic wheels turning.

As you can see from the above, socialists love mandates. Anytime we see a mandate, we can assume that it is necessary because people would behave otherwise without it. They want us all to behave in the same way. This takes coercion, as we are all different and want different things. We will all do the same thing only if we are forced, and to most socialists, this is okay. This produces law after law and regulation after regulation that interferes with the lives of citizens.

You might say all this government involvement is not such a big deal. But it is a big deal when it is happening all over in so many areas, and at a significant cost. Governments interfere with commerce and then pass the cost and inconvenience on to the consumer. You might ask why California has some of the highest gas prices in the nation. It is primarily because of government interference in the marketplace. We all want a clean environment, but we also want to be able to get to work and pay the rent.

Fossil fuels served as a catalyst for us to move from the horse-and-buggy age to the industrial age. They have been enormously beneficial to US and world economic development. Fossil fuel–generated electricity moved us into the digital age. Our nation is making tremendous progress with clean energy, although much of the clean energy today is not so clean. Just a reminder: every new technology must be created and developed, and this can also be a messy process. Fossil fuels played a vital role in the economic development of the US and the world, and they will continue to do so.

Many types of government interference in the marketplace go beyond environmental regulations and delve into the economic decision-making process. This generally leads to a misallocation of resources and higher costs. It also leads to a change in human behavior. Let the market work, and in the long run we will all be better off.

Government leaders come and go, but the citizens of our states are stuck with the results and consequences of their policies. Most often, citizens are also stuck with the bill. More taxes, more regulations, and more statehouse control will never usher in economic nirvana. It will, in fact, take us further from it. Voters, be alert. As we discussed, the economic death wish appears to be alive and well as evidenced by economically reckless state policies. There is also the risk that some of these destructive state policies can find their way onto the national stage.

The idea that we can allow governmental leaders to pass law after law affecting the economic marketplace without damage is unreasonable. The marketplace works; it sets prices based on supply and demand, it allocates goods and services, and it is more productive than any alternative system of economics. Whenever we interfere with the market, bad things happen. The prices end up too high, resulting in surpluses, or they end up too low, resulting in shortages. You can't mess with prices without unintended consequences.

Some US states are learning a hard lesson. High taxes, oppressive business regulations, and the high cost of living in many states are causing citizens to change their state of residence. This is also happening with businesses, which are fleeing to more accommodative areas. However, the economic death wish continues because the people in control stay in control. They think they are enlightened, but they are simply rearranging the deck chairs on the *Titanic*.

The only cure is to elect leaders who exhibit common sense, support practical economic approaches, and understand the real world we citizens live in every day. Maybe you need to get involved.

CHAPTER 10

MODERN MONETARY THEORY

Governments like the idea of printing money. In fact, so do counterfeiters. Printing money captures the imagination and can prove to be an exciting experience. In most cases, unfortunately, it proves *too* exciting. A counterfeiter can print one too many bills, and governments can get carried away with money-printing frenzies that inevitably lead to economic catastrophes. As noted in chapter 4, Milton Friedman is well known for stating: "Inflation is always and everywhere a monetary phenomenon."[1] Repeatedly, history has proven him right.

Printing bills sounds as though the magic money tree and the free lunch have arrived. The German Weimar Republic resorted to this process in the early 1920s to service the massive debt incurred during World War I and to meet the financial sanctions imposed on the nation by the victorious Allies. The result? The collapse in the value of the mark. To indicate the magnitude of the inflation, a loaf of bread in Germany that cost 160 marks in 1922 cost 200 billion marks by the end of 1923.[2]

<table><tr><td>

Hyperinflation in the German Weimar Republic

"The government had to print million-mark notes, then billion-mark notes. By November 1923 one U.S. dollar was equivalent to 1,000 billion (a trillion) marks. A wheelbarrow full of money couldn't buy a newspaper. Shopkeepers couldn't replenish their stock fast enough to keep up with prices, farmers refused to sell their produce for worthless money, food riots broke out, and townspeople marched into the countryside to loot the farms. Law and order broke down. The German attempt at democracy had been completely undermined. Conspiracy theories sprouted, and extremist political views became acceptable. Ultimately, hyperinflation enabled Adolf Hitler to gain power."[3]

</td></tr></table>

Nations still like to print money today. Take Venezuela, for instance. The actual rate of inflation in 2021 was an astounding 1,588 percent.[4] The problem with printing more money than the economy needs for consistent economic growth is that it tends to get out of hand. There always seems to be some pressing issue that requires more money than is currently available. An irresponsible or corrupt central government can then trot out the printing presses and go to town. It appears to work for a while, until everyone realizes what is happening. The day of reckoning approaches as the monetary unit loses value. It can get so bad that no one wants to hold the currency. Employees might want to be paid daily so they can rush to the grocery store before prices go up. Economists refer to this as hyperinflation: monetary inflation occurring at a very high rate. Rates of inflation of 40–50 percent per month generally qualify as hyperinflation. In most of these cases, the rate is accelerating.

When this happens, the economic and social order of the country begins to break down. Loss of productivity, general social unrest, and a loss of confidence in government authorities begins to occur. It is a situation that nations should avoid at all costs. In addition, citizens begin to flee the country in search of a more stable social and economic order. We are seeing some of this at the US southern border.

Nations find themselves in this predicament in multiple ways. For Germany after World War I, debt repayment and payments to the allies contributed to the problem. For Venezuela, running the printing presses and keeping the powerful in power led to a monetary mess. In many instances, previous borrowing can lead to money printing in order to pay the principal and interest on debt incurred by a national government. It is too easy to borrow when times are good, but painful to repay when times are bad. We can find this to be true personally as well as nationally.

Without getting into the more complex details of Modern Monetary Theory, it is important to consider that this theory takes a flexible view regarding the creation of debt and money printing. Unquestionably, a government can be sure it does not default on its debt, as it can simply print the money to pay interest and principal. What the value of the money might be at that time is altogether another matter. The primary limitation on all this borrowing and spending is the rate of inflation. As long as it is reasonably under control, according to the theory, the level of debt is not important.

The problem with all of this? Borrowing and spending generally leads to more borrowing and spending. Once started, it is hard to slow the process. New government programs that get created must then be funded (keeping in mind that most "new" government programs become "old" government programs that never go away, regardless of their effectiveness), and new beneficiaries are created who want to continue to be beneficiaries.

Modern Monetary Theory

The essential message of Modern Monetary Theory (MMT) is that there is no financial constraint on government spending as long as the country is a sovereign issuer of currency and does not tie the value of its currency to another currency. Both Canada and the US are examples of countries who are sovereign issuers of currency. In principle, being a sovereign issuer of currency endows the government with the ability to borrow money from the country's central bank. The central bank can effectively credit the government's bank account at the central bank for an unlimited amount of money without either charging the government interest or, indeed, demanding a repayment of the disproportionately large share of government bonds compared to previous years, which has led some observers to argue that the governments in Canada and the United States are practicing MMT.[5]

In the US today, we can easily observe how borrowing can get out of hand. The 2020 pandemic created the $2.2 trillion CARES Act, followed by the final $900 billion Trump stimulus in December of that year and the $1.9 trillion Biden stimulus in March 2021. In addition, a $1.0 trillion infrastructure bill was passed in the spring of 2021. This is a total of $6 trillion in additional spending that was authorized over a 12-month period. With a $3.1 trillion federal budget deficit recorded in fiscal year 2020 (ending September 30 each year) and $2.8 trillion in 2021, this meant the additional stimulus spending added more to the federal debt.[6]

The $739 billion Inflation Reduction Act of 2022 was passed in August of 2022.[7] It was ironically named, as by that time, all the stimulus plus the lingering effects of the shutdowns had generated inflation in the 8–9 percent range. This act included approximately $372 billion in new taxes and $365 billion in new federal spending. There has been a great deal of difference of opinion as to whether or not the act had much to do with inflation reduction.

All of this does look like Modern Monetary Theory in action. So long as inflation is under control, the borrowing and spending can continue. By March 2021, in my opinion, the economy had almost totally recovered from the pandemic. The extra spending could not be justified on the basis of an "economic emergency." It was simply spending for other purposes. By the way, we were not in it alone. Other nations across the globe were doing the same thing, just not with the level of reckless abandon with which we were borrowing in the United States.

At some point, the economic chickens come home to roost, because the economic chickens always come home to roost. Otherwise, we really have discovered a magical money tree and the free lunch. Can we really spend money we do not have and continue to do so with impunity?

It is the Federal Reserve System's job to call a halt to this process. The Fed can loan funds to the Treasury, but this process has a limit. We are, in effect, *financing our own borrowing.* It is called *monetizing the debt.* This is a government-created money tree. It will only last so long, and then the house of cards comes tumbling down.

When inflation becomes a problem, which it always does, the Federal Reserve will not only have to quit increasing the growth of the money supply, but it will have to reduce the rate of growth (leading to higher interest rates). This very situation happened in the early 1980s to deal with the serious inflation that built up during the '70s. Inflation subsided, but only after a nasty recession in 1981–82.

We are living in a dream world if we think this can just go on and on. When sustained inflation occurs, a responsible Federal Reserve will take action. Of course, it is always better not to let it get started in the first place. As in the early 1980s, this slows the inflation rate—but it also generally leads to a recession. There is no magic money tree or free lunch here. If the good times are too good, the bad times are going to be bad. A nation should never let inflation get out of control. Just ask Venezuela. This is why the Federal Reserve should not get involved in the political landscape. It simply needs to do what is best for the economy, regardless of the political fallout.

The US faced another inflation spiral in 2021–2022 resulting from the stimulus and general money-spending together with the economic fallout from the shutdowns. This created a serious inflationary environment. In the summer of 2022, the YTD inflation rate reached a peak of 9.1 percent.[8] As a result, Fed Chairman Jerome Powell announced interest rate increases that continued into 2023. The chickens had come home to roost, and it was time to pay the piper.

A word to the wise: always keep an eye on the Fed. It will help you read the economic tea leaves and assist you in making wise decisions ahead of events. Another word to the wise: don't follow the crowd chanting the mantra of endless money-printing as a viable solution to fiscal challenges. Remember, the crowd is always right, until it is wrong. The only thing on the money tree is really leaves.

CHAPTER 11

THE DEBT TRAP

IN 2020–2023, AS A RESULT OF OUR REACTION TO THE PANDEMIC, the US stacked up new debt in the trillions. As a result, I have often heard the questions "How much is too much?" and "When will we reach our limit?"

At the end of the US fiscal year 2019, the national debt was $22.719 trillion, which was 107 percent of the nation's Gross Domestic Product. By the end of fiscal year 2022, the debt was $30.824 trillion and 123 percent of the GDP.[1] The government's response to the 2020 pandemic put the national debt increase on steroids. The massive federal spending packages during the pandemic produced the largest short-term increase in the national debt since World War II. In 2020, the Congressional Budget Office provided a projection of the fiscal landscape of federal deficits, debt, spending, and revenue if the current laws on the books did not change. As you can see below, it displayed an alarming trend in the wrong direction:[2]

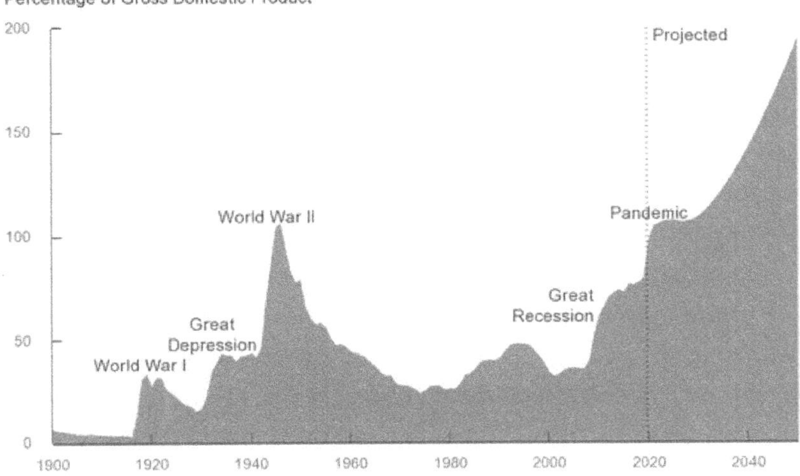

The Congressional Budget Office 2020
Long-Term Budget Outlook.

Prosperous nations and individuals alike can normally handle quite a bit of debt, if they can service it. By this I mean keeping the bondholders happy with regular interest and principal payments. Even if creditors have some concerns about future creditworthiness, they will generally be happy if the cash keeps coming in. When the cash stops flowing, trouble begins. For individuals, repaying debt generally means repaying both interest and principal in some reasonable fashion. This can be a serious drain on anyone's budget. Individuals who end up with a debt problem can't just ignore it and hope it goes away. There is a definite limit. When it is reached, the party is over.

However, with the US federal government, interest payments are the main thing. Of course, maturing bonds must be paid off, but the principal due is normally refinanced by issuing more bonds. In this way, Uncle Sam avoids having to reduce the principal, and in the process, generally ends up increasing the total debt outstanding by issuing more bonds than those actually paid off. This is *not* something we can do individually.

As interest payments eat up a larger and larger portion of the federal budget, trouble looms on the horizon. Governments are generally loath to cut spending due to the political consequences. Therefore, the tendency is to resort to the money-printing option to keep the house of cards intact. This is inflation quicksand. The more you struggle, the deeper you sink. This is precisely how nations wind up with serious inflation (or even hyperinflation), as discussed earlier.

Nations, and individuals too, can handle a lot of debt. There is no rule of thumb that will tell us how much is too much. In Japan, the national debt is consistently much higher in relation to the economy compared to the United States. For example, the Japanese national debt was 218 percent of GDP in 2022.[3] In the US, the national debt topped over $32 trillion (2023) and continues to escalate.[4] However, unlike Japan, the US debt is only about 124 percent of the GDP. Compared to Japan, which is currently handling its debt, the US has a lot of room to expand its borrowing. This means we are not yet near the point where we are reaching any kind of limit. Regrettably, this very fact is leading US authorities to be quite cavalier about the amount of debt we are stacking up.

In addition to the current annual budget, the US government has made a lot of promises over the years, and the cost of keeping these promises is going to be quite significant. Medicare, Medicaid, Social Security, national defense, and other programs will need to be funded at the same time the level of interest payments will be increasing as total debt increases.

There is no longer any serious talk about balancing the federal budget. The only real efforts being made aim to keep the annual budget deficit level somewhat under control. Over the past three years (2020–2023), the US added $7.3 trillion to its national debt.[5]

At this point, as I suggested, we can handle it, but we are moving in a dangerous direction. The pressure for higher taxes generally accompanies a growing national debt. Higher taxes shift funds from productive pursuits in the private sector to the government decision-making process, which usually leads to a reduction in the overall productivity of the general economy. The private sector is the goose that lays the golden egg, and it needs to be nurtured. However, a government in search of cash generally holds this objective in stunningly low regard. Its needs come first.

The answer to the question "How much is too much?" is a difficult one. It is not a specific number. The limit will be reached when there is a loss of confidence in the credit authority of the federal government. When or if this happens depends on not only our own financial condition but also on other world events. Since the end of World War II, the US has been the go-to option for stability in investments and our monetary unit. The dollar has been king and continues to be so. However, competition is on the horizon. The European Union and other countries (particularly China), have aspirations of their own. Any financial weakness on our part will give rise to opportunities to wean the world away from reliance on the dollar.

We must keep our financial situation strong and avoid the debt trap. The frittering away of trillions of dollars on utopian schemes leads us in the wrong direction. Remember, no government will ever be able to make us happy. It is simply not within its power.

The framers of the Constitution knew that happiness is up to the citizen. Government's responsibility is to provide a framework for citizens to have the opportunity to chart a course for their individual happiness. We have wandered far afield from this concept, and financial calamity is becoming more of a real possibility for the United States. We must turn this trend around while we can. Thomas Jefferson believed every generation should pay its own debt, and his powerful words should serve as an alarm for the United States today:

> I place economy among the first and most important
> of republican virtues, and public debt as the greatest
> of the dangers to be feared.[6] (Thomas Jefferson)

Thomas Jefferson knew what he was talking about. The ease of racking up public debt by nations is nothing new. It is as old as money itself. It is so easy to pull out the government credit card for the purchase of almost anything. This situation also contributes to government inefficiency. There is hardly ever any pressure to economize or to stretch the dollars as far as possible. In fact, the opposite is true. If the first few billions don't accomplish anything, then more billions just might. At the state and local level there is more pressure to make the expenditures efficient because those governments generally can't borrow just to meet monthly expenditures. The borrowing is usually limited to road projects and other infrastructure expenditures. Not so with the federal government; it can borrow money for anything and everything, and therein lies the problem.

The US is a long way from financial disaster, but other nations, such as Venezuela, have already blazed this trail. And it can be quite painful. As the money printing gets beyond the limit, inflation arrives with a vengeance. There is just too much money chasing too few goods and the nation flounders. This situation can lead to civil disorder and violence and can even result in the overthrow of governments.

It is critical to remember that the United States has enemies. They would like nothing more than to see the US flounder in a sea of debt and interest payments. There is really no such thing as a free lunch. *Someone always pays.*

During the pandemic, we shut much of the economy down. This created an economic disaster and caused the US government to spend six trillion dollars to save the country from the disaster it created. How ridiculous! Those decisions led to a $32 trillion+ national debt in 2023. And what did we get for the $6 trillion? Basically, nothing. We destroyed economic activity and then replaced the economic activity, thus creating significant inflation in the process. The inflation then created interest rate increases, which whacked the housing market and other sectors of the economy and slowed the economic activity back down (after the stimulus had sped it up).

This is how prosperous nations get into financial difficulties. It is a Modern Monetary Theory nightmare. Businesses go broke doing this sort of thing. But governments can just go on and on until the hammer finally drops. The US economy is so large and powerful that we can stack up a lot more federal government debt before our day is done. Unfortunately, this means we can continue to throw money away for years to come. But it also means that when the day of reckoning does come, *it is going to be ugly*. And when that day comes, we cannot expect help from other countries. We will be on our own.

When we have borrowed more than we can manage, there are only two solutions: (1) keep printing money and allow the inflation rate to go through the roof, or (2) default on some or all of the national debt and work out arrangements with creditors. Any of this would destroy our national credit rating. It has happened to many nations before, and it is destructive to the national integrity of a country. Would you be willing to lend money to the Venezuelan government?

The accumulation of debt is both attractive and seductive. A nation can go a long way down this path before hitting the wall. We don't have to pay off the national debt, but we do have to service it and get it under control. Those in charge of the levers of financial power in Washington must set limits on these billion- and trillion-dollar spending bills. Unfortunately, those who think they have discovered the money tree are unlikely to be the authors of this control.

CHAPTER 12

SOCIALISM ON STEROIDS

THE UNITED STATES OF AMERICA WAS FOUNDED ON FREEDOM. THE colonists were sick and tired of the British government's interference in their daily lives. This is the primary reason the Constitution makes it crystal clear that personal freedom is to be prized and protected. Just remember the first ten amendments to the Constitution we discussed in chapter 1. The Bill of Rights was not created for the government. It was created for the *individual* citizen. The concepts of freedom of religion, speech, the press, and assembly, and the right to petition the government for a redress of grievances, are specifically protected, and a Supreme Court was established to be sure neither the executive branch nor Congress could tamper with these specific rights.

When citizens are compelled to do this or that, freedom is compromised. Often, we go along with various compulsions because we believe it to be in the national interest. However, you don't have to read much history to realize this argument has been used countless times over the centuries to limit individual freedom and enhance governmental power. Some really bad things have been justified in the name of the "national interest" and the "common good."

I am not sure why this happens, but prosperity seems to bring out the socialists in a nation's population. We see it in America today, particularly in some of our most prosperous states and also in many of our colleges and universities. When things are good and resources are plentiful, leaders tend to lean toward policies that run counter to common sense because of a nation's wealth. Big money attracts socialists like a bear to honey.

> Money is power, and socialists like both, especially if it is their power and your money.

It would be great if ardent socialists applied their talents and energy in the private sector to actually *produce something of value.* Unfortunately, this rarely happens. They want to use government to accomplish their objectives. And then, ironically, they want those in the private sector to continue to produce so revenue flows to the government to fund their pet projects. Somehow, they think the private sector will just keep humming along in spite of a mammoth level of regulations and taxes. Recall that government actions tend to result in private reactions to these actions. As a result of new regulations and taxes, behaviors change.

Those who love big government are never content. They always want more. Just one more government program, one more agency, and one more department. And then, one more initiative, one more regulation, one more dictate, and one more tax. And once they get "more," they want "bigger and better." There is no limit to the appetite of those who run government and prosper from its growth.

> Socialism cannot exist without a large and coercive government.

> Capitalism can.

All of this requires billions and trillions of dollars and millions of employees. All the while, courtrooms are backlogged with cases that take years to settle. Highways are crowded and peppered with potholes. Crime is out of control in some areas of the country, and civic services are too often known for poor quality.

Socialist programs take resources away from essential services critical for the functioning of an efficient and productive economy. This is a reminder that although resources are scarce, socialists think they're not. They genuinely believe they can impose their ideas on the economy, society, and individuals, and things will always get better. They understand neither the process nor the reality of production. It is *production* that creates wealth, not government programs.

Some socialists want the US to mimic Europe. Why would we want to do that? The high-tax, sluggish economies of most of Europe are not very attractive. Many of these nations were great empires back in the day but possess scant economic or military power today. Today they are infamous for high taxes. For example, France has a national sales tax (cleverly applied as a "value-added" tax to be less visible to consumers) and also a top income tax rate of 45 percent.[1] In 2021, the United States had a tax-to-GDP ratio of 24.5 percent.[2] By comparison, Denmark had a tax-to-GDP rate of 46.3 percent, Norway 39.9 percent, and Sweden 42.9 percent.[3] Socialists frequently point to these numbers to argue that we are undertaxed here in the United States. What a ridiculous idea.

I will never forget a visit to Denmark where a personable tour guide led us through Copenhagen and frequently commented on all the free things available. He declared we should enjoy it, all courtesy of him. He remarked over and over again, "It's on me." He then reminded us of the steep level of taxes he paid to make all the services possible and "free" to us. You could tell it was an irritating issue with him.

Here's the choice: we can turn most of our paycheck over to government and let it provide the services (some of which we will use and many of which we will never use), or we can keep most of our paycheck and choose our own services. Socialists want the government to provide the services. Freedom-loving people like to do their own thing.

It is sobering to see college students' growing support and

enthusiasm for socialism. It is quite puzzling, because these students are tomorrow's employees and will have to pay for it all. The "free lunch" virus seems to permeate our society. It reminds me of a quote from Louisiana Senator Russell Long, the late chairman of the Senate Finance Committee, who said, "Don't tax me. Don't tax thee. Tax the fellow behind the tree."[4] Taxes are always sold to the population as not affecting them. They are nearly always sold as taxing *someone else.*

This is exactly the way the income tax was sold to the population and ratified in 1913.[5] It was only supposed to impact the rich. That's not exactly the way it worked out. The tax brackets were not indexed to inflation until Reagan did it in 1981 with the Economic Recovery Tax Act.[6] Over prior years, price-level increases turned "them" into "us." Incomes rose, but the tax bracket levels did not, thus eating into lower- and lower-income levels. The socialists of the time loved it as the money poured into Washington. Additionally, monthly withholding constituted a clever approach that made the tax less objectionable to pay rather than an annual bill. Can you even imagine what would happen if every American worker brought home their full paycheck and then had to write a check back to the government every time for income tax withholding? If you think the income tax is just for the rich (as it was initially sold to the American people), just take a moment to investigate and compare your gross pay and your net pay on next month's payroll statement.

As the US continues to incur large federal deficits, the idea of a value-added tax will undoubtedly be floated in the future. Basically, it is a national sales tax. However, it is craftily disguised because it is collected behind the scenes at each level of production. Thus, it will not show up on your bill when you check out at the discount or grocery store. You will pay the tax, you just won't recognize it as a tax. When my daughter Beth Anne ran for US Congress in 2010 and 2012, she often explained the value-added tax as "the sneaky tax" because it's "hidden" and collected at the various levels of production. It's never spelled out on your receipt at the point of purchase, but you will feel the pinch because the overall cost of products and goods will be higher for all consumers.

A value-added tax would be a giant step toward mimicking European nations who have already moved in this direction and have expanded their government's percentage of the economy as a result. In many US states, we already pay sales taxes at the state level. This is precisely where the sales tax *should* be—at the state and local level, where most of the needs are and where citizens can more successfully control where the money goes and how it is spent. Again, this is an example of federalism where the states have taxing power, and that is a good thing.

Remember the Tenth Amendment to the Constitution. This allows the populations of each of our fifty states to have a say about taxes and how government money is spent. Because we live in a free country with open mobility between the states, Americans are free to relocate to any state they feel provides the least burdensome tax structure and where they feel they get the most value for the taxes they pay. Citizens have the freedom to move to states with policies that match their principles and beliefs. The sovereign power of our states is a significant barrier to socialism because it allows for variety. Socialists don't like variety. They want us all to march to the beat of the same drummer—the central government drummer.

In 2021 we witnessed serious resistance by several states to the grand decrees from the federal government about how to handle the pandemic. Many of the states did not want to comply with some of the pronouncements coming out of the Centers for Disease Control. They adopted different policies, and they were on solid legal grounds.

State sovereignty is important, and each state needs to be able to craft different policies. The Constitution grants serious powers to the states in the Tenth Amendment, and these powers must be protected. Just a reminder: the federal government's thirst for power and money will never be quenched. Whatever amount of power, money, and control it has, it will always want more power, money, and control. Socialists think this is a good thing, because they really do believe a concentrated, powerful, and controlling federal government is necessary to direct the actions of people and businesses.

The problem is, there is yet to be one single socialist government (as well-funded as it may be) that has succeeded in remedying injustice, eradicating poverty, stopping crime, or eliminating economic disparity. If anything, the redistribution of private wealth to a central government produces one major outcome: citizens have less power, less money, and less control, and government entities have more of all of it.

State sovereignty is a powerful buffer against a federal concentration of power that eats into personal freedom. Our founders brilliantly designed this system with the individual citizen in mind. Think about it. In most states, it is not at all unusual for citizens to have consistent access to their government officials. Mayors and members of the city council are highly visible and present at local activities such as sporting events, community festivals, civic club lunches, local productions, Sunday morning church, and school events. They show up at events because if they don't, they most likely will draw an opponent in the next election who will be more engaged in the community and connected to citizens. It is also not unusual, especially in smaller states, for citizens to literally run into the governor at the county fair or at a local chamber of commerce dinner. The point is that state and local government is simply more accountable to citizens than the federal government because it is closer to the people.

Another incredible benefit of our form of government includes citizens having the freedom to change their address for *any* reason: a new job, proximity to family, better opportunities, a different climate, health needs, or to simply be in a place with policies reflecting their principles and beliefs. As mentioned earlier, the United States of America has open borders between the states. Truly open. No checkpoints, no gates, and no guards keeping track of who's coming and going across state lines. Open! Not only open, but wide open with "Welcome to Our State" signs and visages of hospitality greeting travelers as they cross state lines.

Not only are Americans free to travel unrestricted state-to-state; they are free to pack up and move between the states at any point and as many times as they choose to do so. They don't get questioned, interrogated, or quizzed. They simply pack up the car and make a move. This is a strength of living in a free country where states are sovereign and have their own constitutionally protected power and authority. Not only do citizens benefit individually and collectively from the benefits of state sovereignty, but the nation as a whole is stronger and more vibrant as well.

The federal government has its playground. The individual states have their playgrounds. Each state is different and empowered to have its own policies within the limits of the Constitution. Those states that want to practice socialism have a certain amount of power to do so. US citizens who don't like that idea have the power to move to communities that are more freedom-oriented. All American citizens are free to live in the state that fits with their personal beliefs. Again, no questions asked. This is a powerful difference maker for the United States. We don't all have to be the same. We can be different. States can be different and have different tax rates, different regulations, and different policies. Socialists want us all to be the same. They want us to be like they want us to be, and they want to use government power to ensure it works out that way. The sovereignty of the states flies in the face of this idea. The Tenth Amendment promotes both freedom and diversity on a national scale and wars against conformity. It is one of the unique factors that makes the United States powerful and special. It also explains why the US is so attractive to the rest of the world and why so many freedom-loving people want to come here.

> If you want to know how people feel, ordinary people feel, about differences, you ask, how people vote with their feet.[7] (Milton Friedman)

Unfortunately, people in many parts of the world cannot vote with their feet. They are stuck. The citizens of Cuba and North Korea have very limited mobility. These countries have to control out-migration, or few would stay. It is not a pretty picture. Across the globe, people risk life and limb to escape to places offering a better life. We can see this every day on the southern border of the United States. People are attracted to freedom and opportunity and repelled by poverty and repression.

I remember visiting with my daughter-in-law's grandfather and listening to his experience with autocratic socialism of two different types. Mr. Frank Koribanic was born in Czechoslovakia and suffered through World War II as a teenager. In fact, he was wounded in an Allied bombing raid and patched up by a German military doctor. And of course, after German control came the Russians. As a young man, he was able to escape from Soviet control to West Germany after the conclusion of World War II. Somehow, he was able to join the US Army there, which opened a world of opportunities for him. He later immigrated to the United States and ultimately became a successful entrepreneur in El Paso, Texas.

He described to me his race across the border and being spotted and shot at by border guards as he made his escape. He recalled hearing bullets whizzing by as he ran for his life and leapt over creeks and obstructions in his desperate bolt for freedom. He did not want fascism or communism. He wanted freedom, and he risked his life to get it.

Any nation that must guard its border to prevent citizens from leaving has a problem. Let's hope we never have to do that in the United States. What we do see today is a significant number of US citizens leaving some states for others. Most of the states they are leaving have governments hostile to capitalism and personal freedom. Some of those same states (and cities) are now beginning to realize that the socialism attraction has its downside.

CHAPTER 13

PICKING WINNERS AND LOSERS

CAPITALISM IS A TOUGH TASKMASTER. INDIVIDUALS AND ENTERPRISES either compete, or they don't. It is sort of like professional football. You either compete, or you don't. The same standard works for players and coaches alike. If you want to play in the NFL, you must compete. If you don't—you're out. The result is a tremendous level of competition on the field of play. Fans pay dearly to witness the competition, and millions watch from all over the world. Competition produces results. When you attend a packed stadium and become part of a thrilling and exciting game, you get to see the results of this process firsthand. Of course, players and coaches must play by the rules. They get penalized or tossed from the game if they don't pay attention to the way the game is to be played.

It is like that in a capitalist free-market economy. Workers and managers must produce if they are going to be successful. Buildings must be constructed properly. Automobiles must be built to last. Machinery must run well. Products must provide the promised benefit. If they don't, consumers will respond. Restaurants that produce mediocre food and provide poor service will not survive. Retail outlets that don't have what you want or provide lackluster service will get crossed off your list. We want what we want, we want it at a reasonable price, and we want it fast. For that to happen, people must work productively, efficiently, and hard.

The American work ethic has historically been one of the key ingredients that helped make the United States the economic superpower it is today. The general population recognizes that work is the key, and they are prepared to work hard and often. We don't take naps in the middle of the afternoon and are frequently willing to work another hour before leaving for the day. As a general norm, we don't come into work late, and we don't leave work early. We are prepared to go the extra mile when necessary. We are willing to put in extra hours, effort, and enthusiasm. This contributes to America's greatness. I cannot count the times people have gone above and beyond to help me or my organization with a pressing matter. The American work ethic has been a shared norm without the corruption of bribes at all levels, which are not just common but epidemic in some parts of the world. Previous generations pounded the work ethic into their children. Make no mistake, young people knew they had to work if they wanted to make it in the world. Some would make the commitment to work, and some would not. Ultimately, the winners and losers were chosen by the individuals themselves, not by society.

This time-tested formula for progress got rattled by the Great Depression. Americans grappled with an economic disaster, allowed to happen by the Federal Reserve System, that was beyond the control of the individual. Work simply *vanished* for millions of Americans. The resulting bailout efforts by the federal government fostered the idea that citizens could look to the government for their survival and even success. This was the first time this had happened in the US, and the effects have been both far-reaching and permanent. The national paradigm and mindset changed. Americans began to think that government, particularly at the federal level, should be involved significantly in the lives of its citizens.

Some programs enacted during the 1930s turned out to be quite beneficial to the economy. The Securities Act of 1935, Securities Exchange Act of 1934, Social Security Act of 1934, Federal Deposit Insurance Corporation Act of 1933 (Glass-Steagall),[1] and Banking Act of 1935 provided an important new framework for banking, investing, and retirement activities.[2] The long list of other programs primarily provided for government assistance for a wide variety of areas such as relief, public works, farm assistance, public safety, housing, and labor law. The list is extensive and created significant involvement of the federal government in almost every facet of American life and the economy.

Following is just a partial list of the first "New Deal" programs:[3]

- Emergency Banking Relief Act (1933)
- Civilian Conservation Corp (1933)
- Agricultural Adjustment Act (1933)
- Tennessee Valley Authority Act (1933)
- National Industrial Recovery Act (1933)
- Public Works Administration (1933)
- Securities Exchange Act (1934)
- National Housing Act (1934)

The Second New Deal followed in 1935–38. It involved a greater level of involvement of the federal government than the first and included the following:[4]

- Works Progress Administration (1935)
- National Labor Relations Act (1935)
- Social Security Act (1935)
- Fair Labor Standards Act (1938)

These Acts and many more dramatically increased the federal role in the life of the economy and its citizens. Some of these Acts were declared unconstitutional, but some of them are still in existence today such as:

- Federal Deposit Insurance Corporation
- Federal National Mortgage Association

- National Labor Relations Board
- Securities and Exchange Commission
- Social Security Administration
- Soil Conservation Service
- Tennessee Valley Authority

All this legislation, followed shortly by the outbreak of World War II and wartime emergency powers, enabled the federal government to get even more involved in the economy. This period, from 1929 until 1945, dramatically changed the way Americans looked at the role of the federal government. Simultaneously, the federal income tax created an unprecedented "money-flow pipeline" straight to Washington. It is interesting that much of this was the result of a depression created by massive bank failures and a dramatic decline in the money supply during a time when cash was king. Tragically, it could have been avoided.

Americans strongly support assistance for those who cannot be gainfully employed or who have become unemployed through no fault of their own. There are many areas where federal or state involvement can strengthen a free-market economy and provide necessary assistance to its citizens (unemployment compensation as an example). It is much like referees in an athletic contest. They are essential to a good and fair game. However, when referees get involved in the game itself, the outcome can be changed. Done right, the playing field is prepared, the boundaries are marked, and the officials are there to ensure the players follow the rules. Beyond that, let the players play. That is where the magic happens and where skilled athleticism is displayed.

Similarly, our governmental authorities should be primarily concerned with providing an environment for economic growth and development, not trying to manage or control it. When legislation is designed, invariably there are those who attempt to tailor it to benefit themselves or their organizations. We must remember the old statement that an elephant is a horse designed by a committee. Or that watching legislation being designed is like watching sausage being made. Legislation usually seems to be adorned with prodigious rules and regulations written by those who may or may not know what they are doing. These rules can frequently make economic activity more difficult or change the decision-making process entirely.

As in an athletic competition, the government should be the referee and not be picking winners and losers. Winners and losers should be picked by the participants themselves. The hard worker should prosper more than the slacker. This is fair and right. Diligence should be rewarded. I certainly know that the unexpected can figure into the equation, but industrious individuals should be given the free and fair opportunity to prosper.

As a nation, we have lost some of our toughness. Life is challenging and can't be approached with a timid attitude. There are successes and failures, and we must meet them head-on. There is a modern tendency to want to protect everyone from everything, and this is just not possible. Many citizens have the attitude that if someone is winning, then they are taking away from someone else and must be stopped. It is what I call the apple pie concept. For those of us who love apple pie, it is terrible to see the pie on the Thanksgiving table begin to disappear before we have gotten our second piece or even our first. The number of slices is limited. If too many get a slice, then someone else may not get to enjoy this delicious dessert.

This is the way most socialists see the economic world. The economic pie is finite. It must be sliced up in equitable pieces, and those in power get to determine what constitutes equity. Socialists tend to focus on slicing up the current pie instead of focusing on how to *bake more pies*. In autocratic societies, that is basically how it works. There is one pie, and the size of the pie is not very big to begin with, and so everyone strives to slice the pie so they get the biggest piece. This means a lot of citizens get left out or only get a sliver of a slice, or maybe only get to lick the empty pie pan.

In capitalism, the concentration is not on the size of the pie *today*. It is on how to increase the size of the pie *in the future.* Moreover, the focus is on how to provide an environment where it's conducive to *bake more pies* for everyone. This is supply-side economics. Increasing the supply of most anything will result in lower prices and more stuff to spread around. Government is at its best when it strives to provide an environment where the economy grows rapidly so there are more pies, and everyone's share of the pie is bigger. The idea is to produce so much that there's plenty to go around, if you are willing to work. This is the essence of economic prosperity.

Now, some are better at producing goods and services than others. This is just part of life. There are others who don't want to make the effort to be particularly productive. That is their choice. Does society owe someone a living if they are not *willing* to make the effort themselves? Socialists generally answer this question with a yes. The problem with saying yes is answering the following question. "Where does the help come from?" The answer: from those who produce goods and services—the producers, makers, creators, and entrepreneurs. This is going to take coercive activity, and coercion is an enemy of freedom.

Let the marketplace determine the winners and the losers. If it does, there are going to be a lot more winners. Why? Because the necessity of being productive gets us out of bed in the morning and creates the drive to get with it, and when we do, good things happen.

I will never forget a businessman friend of mine telling me about how he hired a very long-term and productive employee for his company. He drove by a highway crew each day and noticed that one of the employees always seemed to be working more than the others. One day, he just couldn't resist and stopped and visited with the worker. After a brief conversation, he asked: "Would you like another job?" The worker said yes, and the good result is history. This gentleman became a long-term employee at my friend's company. That's the way it works. Productive employees get additional opportunities either in their present employment or a new one.

If we are taught that being productive doesn't matter very much, we lose our reason to strive, put in additional effort, and go the extra mile. This is the "everyone gets a trophy" mentality. It sounds good to some, but it reduces the drive for excellence and reinforces the tendency of others not to bother with the production part.

Competition is tough stuff! But the goal here is to maximize the production of the population of a nation, and even the world. If this occurs, there is going to be less poverty, less discrimination, a higher general standard of living, more opportunity, and more freedom. There is only one system throughout human history that has shown it is capable of doing all this, and *it is capitalism*.

IN DEFENSE OF CAPITALISM

It is becoming evident today that capitalism needs defending. Those who would lead us toward other economic systems are both vocal and dedicated. We must speak up and promote what we know to be the most efficient economic system ever discovered. In fact, capitalism just happens naturally if people are left alone to pursue their own self-interest.

Capitalism and freedom are inseparable. You can't have true freedom with any other economic system. Milton Friedman defended this concept in his book *Capitalism and Freedom* when he stated, "History suggests that capitalism is a necessary condition for political freedom." Capitalism provides the landscape for political freedom, economic freedom, and individual freedom.[1] Malcom Forbes Jr. echoed this sentiment in 1993 when he stated, "Capitalism is the real enemy of tyranny."[2]

Merriam-Webster defines capitalism as "an economic system characterized by private or corporate ownership of capital goods, by investments that are determined by private decision rather than by state control, and by prices, production, and the distribution of goods that are determined mainly by competition in a free market."[3]

As I noted in chapter 2, the great economist Adam Smith first developed the concept of the "invisible hand" which operates in free-market economies. This invisible hand is self-interest and drives all of us to work to promote our own best interest and well-being.

Self-interest is simply wanting to improve our own situations, and in so doing we improve the national situation. All of this is possible only if we are allowed the freedom to make our own choices about life and liberty.

Capitalism is misunderstood by many people and even by some of its supporters. Adam Smith presented us with the invisible hand decision-making process, and it has proven vastly superior to the bureaucratic process. However, for the invisible hand to work, an environment of capitalism and freedom must be present.

Too few of our citizens really know what capitalism is all about. As a result, they are ill-equipped to defend it against those who would either dramatically alter it or throw it out altogether.

Please examine the following basic principles of capitalism and free enterprise so you will stand ready to defend free markets and freedom at the drop of a hat. Our economic and personal freedom depends upon this defense.

Principles of Capitalism:
Private Property
Freedom of Enterprise
Competition
Reliance on the Price System (Law of Supply and Demand)
Opportunity for Profit
Limited Economic Role for Government
Entrepreneurship

Private Property

Citizens of any country who cannot own their own property are *not* free, and individual and national productivity will suffer. There is something about owning your own home, land, or business that changes everything about the decision-making process. You may recall from chapter 3 that my colleague and fellow professor, Dr. Zhao, articulated the changes that occurred in China when the decision was made to allow citizens to own some of their own land.[4] Productivity went up, and people moved from hunger to a higher standard of living. Why did this happen? Because people are more concerned about their own property than they are about community property. You might walk right past trash on a random street, but you will probably stop and pick it up if it is on your front lawn. The trash alongside the highway is an indication of the disregard citizens may have for common property as opposed to their own.

The concept of private property is one of the most treasured principles of capitalism. Private property, while a function of freedom, is at the same time a catalyst for efficiency. When you own something, it impacts your decision-making about that asset, whether it is a home, farm, vehicle, land, or business. Free-market societies outproduce non-free-market societies, and they always will. Property needs to remain primarily in the hands of private citizens and private businesses. Without the ability to own their own property, citizens are not free.

Freedom of Enterprise

We here in America take for granted our freedom to enter the occupation of our choice and choose our own jobs and careers. We teach our children they can be what they want, if they are willing to work for it. We tell them they can go into business, and if they work hard, they might become another Sam Walton, Bill Gates, Oprah Winfrey, Mark Zuckerberg, Mary Barra, or Elon Musk. The American dream is the opportunity to reach for the future and to accomplish great things without governmental limitations.

Many citizens of the world are not so fortunate, and even some of the capitalistic nations are limiting personal opportunity with rules, fees, red tape, and regulations. It is important to realize if individuals are operating ethically and legally, and are truly free to operate in business and enterprise, they will also benefit society.

There is a tendency of modern governments, both state and federal, to limit or allow the limitation of the opportunity to enter various trades and professions. Many times, rules and requirements to get certain licenses and certifications can be designed to keep competition down for those inside the professions. We certainly want citizens to be qualified for the jobs they do. However, we often see people who are *certified* to do something but not actually qualified in reality. Ironically, we also often run across those who are *qualified* but not certified for one reason or the other. It is essential we keep the paths to occupations as open as possible so every individual can produce at their highest level. This produces great benefits both for the individual and the nation.

Competition

Economics textbooks tell us competition is the existence of many buyers and sellers who operate independently with the freedom to enter and exit the marketplace as they wish. In addition, in his book *Socialism, Capitalism, and Democracy*, Austrian economist Joseph Schumpeter expounded on a concept called creative destruction with the following descriptions in 1943, and they remain true today:

Creative destruction is the essential fact about capitalism.[5]

- As a matter of fact, a capitalist economy is not and cannot be stationary.
- Capitalism, then, is by nature a form or method of economic change and not only never is but never can be stationary.
- The fundamental impulse that sets and keeps the capitalist engine in motion comes from the new consumers' goods, the new methods of production or transportation, the new

markets, and the new forms of industrial organization that capitalist enterprise creates.

Creative destruction means capitalism continues to change and shift as new products are developed and the consumer moves in ever different directions. It is up to the producers to adjust to the changing market realities. Some industries will prosper, and some will languish. Some companies will be hiring as others are reducing payroll. That's just the way it goes. We don't need to protect industries from competition. They just have to read the handwriting on the wall and make the changes early and quickly enough to survive.

Without competition, consumers will not have the necessary amount of influence to protect themselves in the marketplace. In fact, in free markets, the consumer is sovereign, which is the same as being in control. Even the giant corporations must bow to the consumer. If consumers want blue instead of green, that's what they are going to get.

Many believe government must actively interfere in the marketplace for the consumer to get a good deal. Nothing could be further from the truth, *if competition is present.* People in business will work hard, stay open late, and get up early in their effort to please the consumer. Businesses must satisfy the consumer to stay in business, and the successful ones will always be on their best behavior to get you to be a loyal customer.

Reliance on the Price System (Law of Supply and Demand)

In her book *Democracy: Stories from the Long Road to Freedom*, Dr. Condoleezza Rice recounted a memorable experience when her colleague Mike Boskin (chairman of the Council of Economic Advisors for President George H.W. Bush) presented a lecture to a group of Soviet economists. Under the leadership of Mikhail Gorbachev, the USSR was attempting to transition away from communism and toward a more capitalistic society, and Soviet officials had been sent to learn and understand the precepts of the capitalist system. After one of Boskin's lectures on markets, one Soviet finance minister thanked him for his presentation but displayed a flawed understanding of free markets when he questioned, "There is one thing I don't understand. Who sets the prices?"[6]

He missed the point of the presentation. In free markets, the prices are set automatically by supply and demand. It is important for competition to exist, and if it does, no one has to set the prices. It is automatic.

I was in Moscow just before the fall of the Soviet Union and remember so well the ridiculously low prices set by the government. We could feed our whole delegation at the hotel for the price of one hamburger in the United States. These low prices preordained there would be shortages of basic food stuffs in the nation, and indeed there were.

Prices transmit information. The price system works sort of like a magic machine that provides goods and services in the amount desired, at the time desired, and at the appropriate price. If demand for a certain product is greater than the available supply at the moment, two things will happen. First, the price of the good or service will go up because there are more people wanting to buy than the supply available. This can produce cries of profiteering and calls for government action. But the increase in price is a good thing. It signals to consumers to cut back on their purchases, and at the same time, it signals to businesses to increase production. This is precisely what is needed. As production is ramped up, the price will begin to come down and will soon be at the appropriate price based on the demand for and supply of the product. If government interferes or slaps on price controls, then the shortage will become permanent.

Again, prices transmit important information. For a capitalist economy to function at its most productive level, we *need* the information supplied by the price system. It communicates the reality of economic conditions at any given time. The point is simple: Let the market work.

During the gasoline panic of the late 1970s, government regulation of petroleum prices turned a market adjustment into long lines and shortages of gasoline all over the country. Lines at gasoline stations stretched for miles. In some cases, fights broke out among angry drivers waiting for gasoline. It would have been much better to let the price go where it needed to, and then consumers could decide how much fuel they needed. If a good or service is in shortage, let the price go up. Trying to set a ceiling does nothing to create more of the good or service. In fact, it does the opposite: *it perpetuates the shortage.* The lower price discourages businesses from creating more and encourages consumers to continue to buy. When government gets involved, citizens generally end up burdened with allocation gimmicks or ration tickets, none of which can be fairly administered. In 1979, it involved the numbers on your license plate. In several states you could only purchase gasoline every other day depending on whether the last number on your license plate was odd or even. It was a fiasco.

Newly elected President Ronald Reagan abolished price controls in 1981, and the market quickly stabilized as prices declined dramatically from their peak. In a short time, the US went from long lines at the gas station to normal life and reasonable prices for gasoline. As President Reagan stated: "The oil price decline of the 1980s has been a triumph not of government, but of the free market; and not of political leaders, but of freedom itself."[7]

The Opportunity for Profit

Students of economics quickly learn that the factors of production needed to produce goods and services include (1) land, (2) labor, (3) capital, and (4) the entrepreneur. In a free enterprise or capitalistic system, all four of these resources are necessary for products and services to be produced, and they all must be compensated.

A fast-food restaurant must have (1) land on which to locate, (2) employees to prepare the food and keep the business operating, and (3) the capital or equipment to cook the food and house the operation. Additionally, it must have one more thing, or we would have the land, building, and potential employees *but no results*. This critical ingredient is (4) the entrepreneur (aka idea-driven businessperson willing to invest funds, risk failure or bankruptcy, hire and train the employees, and get up in the middle of the night when something goes wrong). The entrepreneur is the glue that holds the free enterprise system together and is the secret weapon of capitalism.

When we receive our paychecks, I assume none of us have recently said, "Please don't pay me, as I don't deserve it." In fact, if our pay did not show up, we would be quite upset. We expect our wages and salaries as just compensation for our labor, and the more the better. The suppliers of capital also expect their return (interest and dividends), and the providers of land expect their rent or the price of the property.

When we watch our favorite sports stars, we are reminded of the tremendous salaries paid for their services. Multimillion-dollar contracts are now routine as teams compete for superstars. It is important to remember that just as sports stars are important to their teams, *entrepreneurs are important to their businesses.* It is not a bad thing that some business owners are well compensated for their services. In fact, the opportunity is there for many of us to go into business, if we are willing to take the risk, work the long hours, make the tough decisions, and take the responsibility for failure as well as success.

I recall reading that when Mikhail Gorbachev visited the US as President George H.W. Bush's guest during the late 1980s, he toured by helicopter to get an overhead view of America. As Gorbachev soared over miles and miles of single-family housing developments, he asked about the process by which the houses came to be built. In the old Soviet Union, it would have taken a massive government program to accomplish such a feat. Most of the citizens of Russia at that time lived in giant, austere apartments, flats, and complexes built by the government.

But the houses in the US seen by Gorbachev were not built by any government. They were constructed by private businesses for private citizens with private money. It was the *entrepreneur* who saw the need, raised the money, organized the construction, hired the workers, and brought these houses into being.

Why did they do it? It was for the possibility of a profit, of course. If any money was left over after the cost of land, labor, taxes, and capital, the rest went to the builder. Sometimes there is a lot left, sometimes none, and sometimes the builder may incur a loss. If the profits are large, more builders will build, and these housing developments will multiply. If the profits are small or losses are suffered, the construction will slow or even stop. Profits perform an essential service for a capitalistic economy, and they are a return for the work and creative talents of the entrepreneur. Without the profits, we would not have the entrepreneur. Without the entrepreneur, we would not have the houses. Without the houses, you and I might not live nearly as well. We also might not have a job that was created because of all the construction. Entrepreneurs create jobs, and profits are the tantalizing incentive the entrepreneur needs to make all this possible.

A Limited Economic Role for Government

Milton Friedman said it best when he asserted, "The greatest threat to freedom is a concentration of power."[8] The founders of the United States had a healthy distrust of the coercive power of government. As we discussed earlier, the oppression of the colonists by the British government was firmly established in the minds of those who framed the American Constitution.

Capitalism and free enterprise tend to be restricted as the governments of nations grow, particularly at the federal or national level. In France, government accounts for roughly 50 percent of the national income, and the national economy is stagnant. In Italy, which has experienced numerous recent recessions, the economy has been struggling for years. France currently ranks 70th worldwide on the Index of Economic Freedom and Italy ranks 86th. By comparison, the United States ranks twelfth.[9] Few would argue that much of the economic difficulties experienced in France and Italy are related to the socialistic nature of the economies. It is also worth remembering that France and Italy were once great empires, but no longer.

Government, of course, has a valuable and indispensable role in providing a stable and safe environment which encourages economic development and freedom. The military, fire departments, police, transportation, and legal system are all essential to the proper functioning of a free enterprise economy. If goods are stolen in shipment, contracts to pay are not honored, or the highways are inadequate or unsafe, the economy will not be able to create the standard of living citizens desire. Government has important things to do, but it does not need to try to run the economy, set wages and prices, or spend large sums on programs that discourage citizens from working.

Governments that drift from their basic functions and push into large-scale interference in the economy produce two significant effects. First, they reduce the efficiency of the free market by introducing arbitrary rules, regulations, and prices into an otherwise commonsense economy. Second, the government drains away valuable resources that should be used to perform its basic functions. Who can argue that law and order has suffered in the United States as the federal government spends billions on projects and activities that make little sense to many citizens, and frequently even harm the economy and society? In the process, Washington has grown to take 23.5 percent of the Gross Domestic Product and has generated a national debt exceeding an unthinkable $30+ trillion. Policymakers often seem to believe there really is such a thing as a free lunch, and all they have to do is print more money anytime they wish to launch yet another government program.

A nation that recognizes private property, values free enterprise, allows competition, relies on the price system, promotes the opportunity for profit, and is dedicated to a limited government role in the economy is a capitalistic or free-market economy. It is these nations that generate economic miracles and lead economic development wherever they are found. Certainly, the United States owes much of its success to the fact it has been largely a capitalist free-market nation for its nearly 250-year history. As former US Senator and economist Phil Gramm of Texas said in 1988: "The genius of the American system is that through freedom we have created extraordinary results from plain old ordinary people."[10]

Entrepreneurship

Economist Joseph Schumpeter viewed the entrepreneur as the "cornerstone of capitalism" and articulated the belief that the "vital force behind capitalism is innovation and the entrepreneur willing to introduce it."[11]

In a free-market society, it is imperative to communicate to a young generation the importance of innovation and idea-creation. Instead of solely focusing on getting a job or finding a job, our conversation should promote the idea of *creating a job.*

+ + +

These principles of capitalism are vital to the preservation of this freedom-embedded economic system that has produced the world's most prosperous and generous nation. These principles are woven into the DNA of capitalism, and it is important we understand and teach these principles to sustain the best of what the capitalist system offers.

It is difficult to believe the world's most powerful and productive economic system needs defending, *but it does*. If we are to be defenders of freedom, we must be defenders of the economic system that upholds that freedom.

CHAPTER 15

CAN CAPITALISM BE SAVED?

HARVARD PROFESSOR AND TWENTIETH-CENTURY ECONOMIST JOSEPH Schumpeter (introduced in the previous chapter) posed an ominous question in Part II of his book *Capitalism, Socialism, and Democracy*: "Can Capitalism be Saved?"[1] Nearly eighty years later, we wrestle with the same question.

Capitalism has consistently proven to be the world's most effective economic system for the creation of economic value. Just compare what you know about South Korea with what you know about North Korea. Is anyone out there driving an automobile made in Pyongyang? What about comparing Havana, Cuba, to Miami, Florida? Cuba is a place where old American automobiles go to die. It is hard to argue logically that any of the various forms of socialism are superior to capitalism and free markets. If a socialist utopia exists, *where is it?* Is it on another planet we have not yet discovered? Has it ever existed?

Does North Korea have an immigration problem? No, because no one wants to get in. They would assuredly have an emigration problem *if people could get out.* However, they will shoot you if you try that. On the other hand, who *does* have a serious immigration problem? The United States. The country practicing capitalism and free markets is the world's number-one population magnet. As testimony, undocumented migrant southwest border crossings into the US were a record 2.76 million in FY2022 alone.[2] Many immigrants risk life and limb and walk hundreds of miles just to get here. They know full well even average Americans have a standard of living and a level of freedom much of the rest of the world only dreams of.

But according to some US political leaders, the US is a hotbed of inequity, discrimination, and oppression. How can this be if millions of people want to come here? Isn't the United States the world's leader in economic and military power? Don't we have a Constitution with a Bill of Rights guaranteeing specific rights and privileges to every American regardless of social standing, economic status, or ethnic background? What is the motivation of those who make such claims? It is important to remember to compare the real with the real. This is what immigrants are doing when they flee other parts of the world in route to the US. They are not looking for utopia but for a better life.

Capitalism, with the application of the rule of law, is vastly superior to other forms of economic activity. The evidence is conclusive. If this is the case, why do so many Americans struggle with the concept of capitalism? Why does the idea of socialism seem to be gaining ground? It is troubling that a significant percentage of college students today favor socialism and are critical of capitalism. Many of these students are attending expensive universities and are there because of the economic power and mobility created by capitalism and enjoyed by their parents. It is concerning that these students will soon be out in the economy and society influencing social, economic, and political decisions.

The direction of civil and political discourse on socialism is also disturbing. In the United States we have an economic system that has created the world's largest middle class and is the earth's most robust exporter of generosity and foreign aid to citizens of other countries. Millions of these countries' citizens dream of coming here one day. Yet many here want to throttle the capitalist system, chip away at the principles that make it work, or even jettison it for something else—primarily, socialism, or worse.

Recall our discussion from chapter 4 on Karl Marx. He encouraged workers to throw off the yoke of capitalists and embark on a search for a socialist utopia. But it was people like Lenin, Mao, and Castro who put his ideas into practice. The results: severe economic and human destruction. This is the primary problem with socialism. It sounds so good, but it does not work so well. It also takes a lot of coercion, and the level of coercion varies with those in charge.

Why does all this escape today's advocates of socialism? It must be they really believe it will work *this time* because *they* will be in charge. If the greedy capitalists can just be stripped of their property and power, life will be tulips and roses. Socialists propose a great variety of ways to bring capitalists and property owners to heel. The estate (death) tax is quite popular, along with high income tax rates for the wealthy. In addition, wealth taxes are now being proposed in the United States, which would amount to the confiscation of private property before the death of the owner. It would be particularly destructive for newly wealthy minorities who have been very successful in the US during the past several decades.

Wealth taxes are being proposed, even though the US Constitution prohibits such an activity (Fifth Amendment). You can't just take property away from citizens because you want to. It is also certainly not in the best economic interest of the nation. The United States has numerous multibillionaires, and some people think that level of wealth is evil. However, most of the value for these wealthy individuals is in the stock of their highly successful companies, many of which they created. They are not just sitting on top of a huge stack of Federal Reserve Notes. These successful enterprises employ thousands of people and produce products and services that make life better for us all. Is it the right of government to take this property away from those who earned and created it? In effect, the proponents of these tax schemes are really saying that wealth is a bad thing. The wealth created by successful corporations and their creators can be tremendous. But this wealth pales by comparison with the power and influence of the US Speaker of the House of Representatives, who controls the budget strings of a $6.2 trillion national budget. This makes Bill Gates, with $112 billion in net worth (2023), seem like small potatoes.[3] It is also important to remember Gates *created* this wealth along with hundreds of thousands of jobs, but the Speaker of the House *acquired* his or her economic power through political activity, taxation, and borrowing.

French economist and writer Frédéric Bastiat wrote about this sort of socialist mindset during the French revolution in 1848, as France was rapidly turning to socialism:

> It is not true that the legislator has absolute power over our persons and property. The existence of persons and property preceded the existence of the legislator, and his function is only to guarantee their safety …. It is not true that the function of law is to regulate our consciences, our ideas, our wills, our education, our opinions, our work, our trade, our talents, or our pleasures. The function of law is to protect the free exercise of these rights, and to prevent any person from interfering with the free exercise of these same rights by any other person.[4] (Frédéric Bastiat)

Bastiat's reference to "our ideas, our wills, our education, our opinions," fits with the direction many see the United States going in recent years. More and more government and regulatory control is being exerted over the freedom of Americans to speak about and do what they want—especially when their views or opinions conflict with the politically correct theme of the moment. Just remember, nothing about this is new, it has all been tried before, all with bad results. It reminds us, as we discussed in chapter 6, that King Solomon was right: "What has been done will be done again; there is nothing new under the sun."[5]

Capitalists create wealth and build companies in which we all like to invest. In addition, they create quality goods and services we need for our daily lives and add to the total production of the United States. Many government leaders like to use the power of government to reallocate wealth and income to the federal budget and federal decision-making. There is a big difference here. One is private decision-making, and the other is public decision-making by elected individuals and bureaucrats.

To keep things in perspective, the US federal budget is larger than the total gross domestic product of Japan and Russia put together. It is spending lots of money, but it always wants to spend more. That's just government. But to spend more, it must tax more or borrow more, or both. These activities can result in the reduction of freedom in an economy.

The founders of this great nation put some wonderful things in the Constitution. However, one thing they forgot was some kind of limitation on the size and intrusiveness of central government. In the Federalist Papers, Alexander Hamilton envisioned that "the general government will at all times stand ready to check the usurpations of the state governments, and these will have the same disposition towards the general government."[6] The checks and balances of the Constitution were brilliantly designed to take care of this. However, it all changed in 1913 when the Sixteenth Amendment (income tax) opened Pandora's box of federal income taxes and ushered in an unstoppable flood of revenue straight to Washington, DC.

For capitalism to survive, *it must first be understood* by the general population. We must promote it in our schools and colleges. As citizens, we must realize capitalism and freedom are joined at the hip just like big government and socialism. Capitalism emphasizes freedom and production, and socialism emphasizes big government and redistribution of existing wealth. Do we really understand this? We must. Our future freedom depends on it.

Good government is essential. It is supposed to make sure highways are built, money is sound, streets are safe, our military is strong, and our freedom of speech is protected. It should not attempt to regulate our lives; we can do that for ourselves, within the law, of course. Back when central government was small, the threat to freedom was small. Now that central government is large, the threat to freedom is large.

If we continue to cede more and more of our income, wealth, and decision-making to central government, we will dramatically reduce our freedom and the efficiency of capitalism. We must teach the next generation about the value of freedom, entrepreneurship, and capitalism. If we fail to do so, we will witness the gradual loss of freedom, competitive advantage, and vitality our economy needs to prosper during the balance of this young century. We need a central government, but we need one that knows its mission (and the boundaries of that mission). This mission is to provide an environment for its citizens and entrepreneurs to prosper. It needs to be the referee but not the coach.

I cut the state governments a lot of slack here. Individual citizens can have more of an impact on their state's leadership than is possible with Washington. We can see this as our fifty states have dramatically different regulatory and taxation policies. This is good. The states which follow commonsense policies will prosper, and those that don't will suffer. Sooner or later the wayward states will see the handwriting on the wall and make changes. We see this today as states make the news with policies that differ dramatically from each other. Good government in our states also serves as a safeguard against the encroachment of the federal government in the lives of citizens. As President Dwight D. Eisenhower stated in 1964, "Our best protection against bigger government in Washington is better government in the states."[7]

I love this quote from John Locke in 1690: "The end of law is not to abolish or restrain, but to preserve and enlarge freedom."[8]

We have strayed far from this concept in our effort to solve every ill known to humankind. What are we thinking? We are on our way to giving away freedom in return for a questionable level of security. In a reply to the governor of Pennsylvania in 1755, Ben Franklin penned a stark warning on this topic by stating, "Those who would give up essential liberty to purchase a little temporary safety, deserve neither liberty nor safety."[9]

Through the years, I often reminded my students:

- When economic freedom is enhanced, personal freedom is enhanced.
- When economic freedom is diminished, personal freedom is diminished.

Socialists believe they can just tax this or that and confiscate property without any consequences. Americans who understand economics know this is not reality. Income taxes have consequences. Regulations have consequences. Wealth and estate taxes have consequences. But all of this is the mother's milk of socialism. The socialists need the revenue to carry out their policies. Without the big government bucks, they die on the vine.

A number of countries have experimented with wealth taxes. For most, the experiment has not worked out too well. Some nations that implemented wealth taxes later repealed them. Only four OECD (Organization for Economic Cooperation and Development) countries today have a wealth tax: Colombia, France, Norway, and Spain.[10] By comparison, in 1960 there were twelve OECD countries with a wealth tax.[11]

Wealth taxes are difficult to administer, generally raise less revenue than projected, and can have a negative impact on wealth creation within the taxing region. As you might imagine, wealth taxes impact decision-making and behavior by those affected by the tax. This decision-making is generally not in the best interest of economic development and growth but in the interest of reducing exposure to the tax. Wealth taxes are promoted by proponents as only affecting the "super-rich." However, it is worth remembering the modern US personal income tax started out in 1913 at 1 percent on income above $3,000 and then up to 7 percent on income above $500,000.[12]

It was also proposed as only for the "super rich." But, if you adjusted these numbers for inflation, the brackets today would be $83,972 and $13,999,408 respectively.[13]

If we had to pay those initial rates adjusted for inflation, that would be fine. However, today, at the lowest income level (see below), the 2022 rate is 10 percent on up to $10,275 of taxable income and then increases on to a top rate of 37 percent. This is a lesson in how tax rates can work. They may start out at a rate that affects *someone else* but before long ends up *affecting you*. There can be little doubt a wealth tax would most likely start out impacting someone else, but in time (and sooner than you think), it would impact you.

The initial (1913) top federal income tax rate of 7.0 percent did not stay at that level for very long. As you can see from the 2022 list below, the situation changed significantly from its humble beginnings. The income tax was instituted as a "tax the rich" idea, but that is certainly not the case today. The brackets were not indexed to inflation until 1981 under the Reagan administration. It was a Republican president and a Democratic Speaker of the House (Tip O'Neill) who made this happen. This simple step saved American taxpayers billions and billions of dollars in taxes. These are dollars which stayed in citizens' pocketbooks, made life better, and enhanced the freedom to spend one's own income.

2022 Income Tax Brackets[14]

	Single Taxpayer	*Head of Household*
10%	Up to $10,275	Up to $20,550
12%	$10,276 to $41,775	$20,551 to $83,550
22%,	$41,776 to $89,705	$83,551 to $178,150
24%	$89,706 to $170,050	$178,151 to $340,100

32%	$170,051 to $215,950	$340,101 to $431,900
35%	$215,951 to $539,900	$431,901 to $647,850
37%	Over $539,900	Over $647,850

Tax rates, whether on income, capital gains, wealth, or sales, can change decision-making and impact human behavior. If the rates get too high, tax avoidance and tax evasion go into high gear. When this happens, people and enterprises may begin to make tax-smart decisions, not business-smart decisions. That is rarely best for the consumer or the nation in general. Tax rates should never be so high that they interfere with commonsense decision-making.

Eventually, the economic system will sag under the burden of taxes and regulations, and economic value creation and employment creation will be negatively impacted. Keep in mind that even when this happens, the socialists are undeterred. They claim if only you would give them more money and more power, they would make it all better. They tend to blame the private sector for the problems and present government as the solution. However, it is usually the government-driven taxes, regulations, and policies that have created the problems in the first place.

Socialists tend to blame private enterprise for society's ills and view profits as the pot of gold at the end of the rainbow. Corporate and business profits are a tempting target for the socialist, as if they are big piggy banks the corporations are hoarding. It is important to remember a corporation is more than a legal piece of paper, a corporate charter. The corporation is really the customers, the employees, and the shareholders. If taxes are increased on a corporation, the customers are likely to pay more, employees will be paid less, and dividends paid to shareholders will likely be less than they would normally be. In addition, there will certainly be fewer after-tax profit dollars to plow back into the business for expansion and improvement. Yes, businesses should pay taxes. But they are not a piggy bank. There is no free lunch here. Pretax corporate and business profits go in only three directions: dividends, corporate reinvestment, and corporate income taxes. The higher the taxes, the less the cash for dividends and corporate reinvestment. It is reinvestment that creates business growth and employment for the company. And it is dividends and corporate profits that encourage citizens to invest in corporations and provide capital for expansion.

Yes, we need essential government services and a revenue stream to support them. However, many government programs have little to do with essential services. In fact, the "defund the police" movement in 2021–22 attacked a very essential service. Without the police, we will not have an orderly society which is a key cornerstone for economic growth and development. We also hear often about new "pie in the sky" national spending initiatives that may have little benefit to society and yet will drain essential resources from the private sector. How much longer can this go on? Where is our common sense?

A new mentality is emerging in the United States: that we can spend trillions of dollars, snap our fingers, and the money simply *appears*. Are we so divorced from reality we think this is sustainable? It takes production to create value. It cannot be created by political leaders snatching it out of thin air with a government credit card.

The generation who survived the Great Depression and won World War II has been replaced by generations who think that just because they *are*, they deserve prosperity. What a bankrupt idea. Each generation must create its own prosperity through perseverance and hard work. Each of us should have the right to life, liberty, and the pursuit of happiness. The law should give us the life and the liberty, but the *pursuit* of happiness is on us.

Another responsibility that is ours is the safekeeping of freedom and the freedom-principled economic system of capitalism, which helps ensure it. As World War II General Douglas MacArthur said, "No man is entitled to the blessings of freedom unless he is vigilant in its preservation." The Greatest Generation did their part. Now it's our turn to do our part.[15]

According to Gallup, only half of college students today view capitalism in a positive light. This is down from 66 percent in 2010. The students' positive view of socialism is now approximately 50 percent compared to 30 percent for baby boomers and traditionalists. However, it is encouraging that for all Americans, there remains a high regard for small business at 97 percent.[16]

The level of college student support for socialism is concerning because they are our future leaders. I have long been concerned that most college students graduate with little or no exposure to market economics. When graduates do not understand the history and causes of inflation, the factors affecting economic growth, and the role of profits in an economy, they can be led astray by a variety of wacky ideas.

I have always appreciated this quote from John Maynard Keynes, and it is certainly appropriate for today:

> Practical men who believe themselves to be quite exempt from any intellectual influence are usually the slaves of some defunct economist. Madmen in authority, who hear voices in the air, are distilling their frenzy from some academic scribbler of a few years back.[17] (John Maynard Keynes)

We who value freedom, the Constitution, free enterprise, capitalism, and personal responsibility need to speak up. It is essential to confront outlandish ideas with facts and reason. We must stick up for what we know works and for what provides the most opportunity both socially and economically. As former US Senator Alan K. Simpson stated, "There is no 'slippery slope' toward loss of liberties, only a long staircase where each step downward must first be tolerated by the American people and their leaders."[18]

Ample evidence exists that capitalism and free markets are the best opportunity for a population to work, produce, and prosper.

Milder forms of socialism are a distant second, and communism and fascism are at the bottom of the rung. We must make certain the next generation knows and understands this. It must be promoted in schools and colleges. It must be taught. This is what education is all about. It is not indoctrination, it is information. It is evidence. It is debate and inquiry. Let people with different views express their positions, *but at least let the capitalism position be presented.* Let the concept be at the table. Let the academic forum be open. Those who value logic and reason will have a difficult time opposing the power, freedom, and logic of capitalism. We must not support economic systems that do not value freedom.

The future is coming. Let's ensure it is a future with freedom. Let's understand economics. Let's understand freedom. And with ever-increasing vigilance, let's understand the *economics of freedom.*

ENDNOTES

Introduction

1   Alfred Thompson Denning, *The Family Story* (London, Boston: Butterworths, 1981), 12–34.
2   M. Harrison and S. Gilbert, *Thomas Jefferson: In His Own Words* (New York: Excellent Books in arrangement with Barnes & Noble, Inc., 1993).

Chapter 1

1   The Declaration of Independence.
2   Ibid.
3   Smith, Adam. *An Inquiry into the Nature and Causes of the Wealth of Nations*, Book V, Chapter II, Part II, appendix to Articles I and II, p. 861, paragraph 12, The Adam Smith Institute.
4   The Declaration of Independence.
5   Teare, R. J., & McPheeters, H. L. (1970). A Report Based on a Symposium on Manpower Utilization in Social Welfare Services.
6   Quoted in Bill Adler, ed., *The Quotable Conservative: The Wit, Wisdom, and Insight of Freedom's Most Passionate Advocates* (Carol Publishing Group, 1996). Quoted from *The Buffalo News*. June 15, 1995.
7   A. Ujifusa, "National School Board Group's Apology for 'Domestic Terrorism' Letter May Not Quell Uproar." October 24, 2021, https://www.edweek.org/policy-politics/national-school-board-groups-apology-for-domestic-terrorism-letter-may-not-quell-uproar/2021/10
8   Quoted in Adler, *Quotable Conservative*. Quoted from *New York Times Magazine*, September 30, 1951.
9   U.S. Supreme Court, *District of Columbia et al. v. Heller*, June 26, 2008. https://www.justice.gov/osg/brief/district-columbia-v-heller-amicus-merits
10 Battles of Lexington and Concord: United States History. https://www.britannica.com/event/Battles-of-Lexington-and-Concord
11 Documents from the Continental Congress and the Constitutional Convention 1774 to 1798. Library of Congress. https://www.loc.gov/collections/continenta

l-congress-and-constitutional-convention-from-1774-to-1789/articles-and-essays/timeline/1764-to-1765/

12 New International Version.

13 C.S. Lewis, *God in the Dock* (Pte. Ltd., 1970). Reprinted with permission.

14 Friedman, Milton. *Capitalism and Power* (Chicago: University of Chicago Press, 1962).

15 From Patrick Henry's Speech to the Virginia House of Burgesses, Richmond, Virginia, March 23, 1775. *Historic American Documents* (Lit2Go Edition). Retrieved June 7, 2021, from https://etc.usf.edu/lit2go/133/historic-american-documents/4956/patrick-henrys-speech-to-the-virginia-house-of-burgesses-richmond-virginia-march-23-1775.

16 "John Adams to Abigail Adams, 7 July 1775," *Founders Online*, National Archives, https://founders.archives.gov/documents/Adams/04-01-02-0160. Original source: Lyman H. Butterfield, ed., *The Adams Papers*, Adams Family Correspondence, vol. 1, *December 1761–May 1776* (Cambridge, MA: Harvard University Press, 1963), 241–243.

17 Harrison and Gilbert, *Thomas Jefferson: In His Own Words.*

Chapter 2

1 Smith, Adam. *Wealth of Nations.*

2 Musk, Elon. Interview, May 2020.

3 Adams, John. National Historical Publications and Records Commission. Founders Online: https://founders.archives.gov/documents/Adams/99-02-02-3102

4 Smith, Adam. *Wealth of Nations.*

5 Cato Institute, Human Freedom Index, https://www.cato.org/human-freedom-index/2021, Ian Vasquez, Fred McMahon, Ryan Murphy, & Guillermina Sutter Schneider.

6 Ibid.

7 Oxford Languages. Oxford English Dictionary: https://www.oed.com/view/Entry/116609?redirectedFrom=mercantilism#eid

8 Smoot-Hawley Tariff Act, United States Senate online: https://www.senate.gov/artandhistory/history/minute/Senate_Passes_Smoot_Hawley_Tariff.htm

9 Huntsman, Jon. https://www.brainyquote.com/authors/jon-huntsman-jr-quotes

10 Smith, Adam. *Wealth of Nations.*

11 Chernow, Ron. Alexander Hamilton. Head of Zeus, Ltd. 2016.

12 Jordan, Terry. *The U.S. Constitution and Fascinating Facts About It.* Oak Hill Publishing Company, Naperville, IL. 2015.

13 Chernow, Ron. Alexander Hamilton. Head of Zeus, Ltd. 2016.

Chapter 3

1   Communism: Karl Marx to Joseph Stalin. https://europe.unc.edu/iron-curtain/history/communism-karl-marx-to-joseph-stalin/

2   Marx, K., and Levitsky, S.L., *Das Kapital: A Critique of Political Economy.* Washington: H. Regnery. 1965.

3   Marx, K., and Engels, F. *The Communist Manifesto.* In Ideals and Ideologies. Routledge, 1848.

4   Brinkley, George. "Leninism: What It Was and What It Was Not." *The Review of Politics*, vol. 60, no. 1, [University of Notre Dame du lac on behalf of Review of Politics, Cambridge University Press], 1998, pp. 151–64, http://www.jstor.org/stable/1408333.

5   Marx, Karl. Communist Manifesto.

6   Zhou, Limount. Interview with Dr. David F. Rankin. July 2021.

7   Vladimir Lenin Quotes. BrainyQuote.com. BrainyMedia, Inc,. 2022. https://www.brainyquote.com/quotes/vladimir_lenin_136421, accessed April 19, 2022.

8   Zedong, Mao. *Problems of War and Strategy.* Online: http://afe.easia.columbia.edu/special/china_1900_mao_war.htm

9   Deutsch, Monroe E. "E Pluribus Unum." *The Classical Journal*, vol. 18, no. 7, The Classical Association of the Middle West and South, 1923, pp. 387–407, http://www.jstor.org/stable/3289233.

10 Vladimir Lenin Quotes. BrainQuote.com. BrainyMedia, Inc., 2022. https://www.brainyquote.com/quotes/vladimir_lenin_153238, accessed April 19, 2022.

11 Locke, John. The Second Treatise of Government. Originally published 1690. New York, NY: Barnes & Noble, Inc. 2004.

12 Ibid.

13 Reagan, Ronald. September 25, 1987. Compiled by Bill Adler. *The Quotable Conservative: The Wit, Wisdom, and Insight of Freedom's Most Passionate Advocates.* Carol Publishing Group. 1996.

14 Buckley, William F. June 30, 1995. The Fresno Bee. Compiled by Bill Adler. *The Quotable Conservative: The Wit, Wisdom, and Insight of Freedom's Most Passionate Advocates.* Carol Publishing Group. 1996.

Chapter 4

1   Federal Reserve Act. Online: https://www.federalreserve.gov/aboutthefed/fract.htm

2   Friedman, Milton. *Free to Choose.*

3   Friedman, Milton. Speech. Free to Choose Network, Milton Friedman teaches monetary policy, https://www.youtube.com/watch?v=6LfUyML5QVY

4   Ibid.

5   Ibid.

6   Arizona Empowerment Scholarship Accounts HB2853, www.azed.gov

7   Friedman, Milton. *Free to Choose.*

8   *Free to Choose* Video Series, Public Broadcasting System. Milton Friedman. https://www.youtube.com/watch?v=f1Fj5tzuYBE

Chapter 5

1   International Monetary Fund. What is Keynseian Economics? Finance & Development, September 2014, Vol. 51, No. 3. https://www.imf.org/external/pubs/ft/fandd/2014/09/basics.htm

2   https://www.fdrlibrary.org/great-depression-facts

3   Ibid.

4   Bureau of Economic Analysis. https://www.bea.gov/resources/learning-center/what-to-know-gdp

5   Barsky, Robert B., and Lutz Kilian. "Do We Really Know That Oil Caused the Great Stagflation? A Monetary Alternative." *NBER Macroeconomics Annual*, vol. 16, University of Chicago Press, 2001, pp. 137–83, http://www.jstor.org/stable/3585363.

6   President Gerald R. Ford's Address to a Joint Session of Congress on the Economy. October 8, 1974. Online: https://www.fordlibrarymuseum.gov/library/speeches/740121.asp

7   https://www.presidency.ucsb.edu/documents/remarks-signing-the-win-consumer-pledge

8   Consumer Price Index, Federal Reserve Bank of Minneapolis. www.minneapolisfed.org

9   National Archives Catalog. Department of Agriculture. Agriculture Adjustment Administration (1933 – 2/23/1942). Organization Authority Record. https://catalog.archives.gov/id/10516302

10   Urquhart, Michael A., and Hewson, Marillyn A., Unemployment Continued to Rise in 1982 as Recession Deepened. Bureau of Labor Statistics. https://www.bls.gov/opub/mlr/1983/02/art1full.pdf

11   Economic Recovery Tax Act of 1981. https://www.congress.gov/bill/97th-congress/house-bill/4242

12   Tax Reform Act of 1986. https://www.congress.gov/bill/99th-congress/house-bill/3838

13 Bureau of Labor Statistics. News Release: Consumer Price Index, March 2022. April 12, 2022. https://www.bls.gov/news.release/pdf/cpi.pdf

Chapter 6

1   Pollack, Sheldon D. "The First National Income Tax, 1861–1872." *The Tax Lawyer* 67, no. 2 (2014): 311–30. http://www.jstor.org/stable/24247751.

2   U.S. Constitution. 16th Amendment

3   Thatcher, Margaret. Interview, *This Week* Thames TV, February 5, 1976. https://www.oxfordreference.com/view/10.1093/acref/9780191826719.001.0001/q-oro-ed4-00010826

4   Kennedy, John F., Commemorative Message on Roosevelt Day, January 29, 1961. https://www.jfklibrary.org/learn/about-jfk/life-of-john-f-kennedy/john-f-kennedy-quotations/commemorative-message-on-roosevelt-day

5   Sowell, Thomas. https://townhall.com/columnists/thomassowell/2012/12/25/random-thoughts-n1473508. December 25, 2012.

6   Solomon. New International Version. Ecclesiastes 1:9.

7   Budget of the U.S. Government, Office of Management and Budget, https://www.whitehouse.gov/wp-content/uploads/2022/03/budget_fy2023.pdf

8   Musk, Elon. Twitter, @elonmusk, October 25, 2021.

9   Musk, Elon. Twitter, @elonmusk, October 28, 2021.

10 Kennedy, John F. Speech. https://english.stackexchange.com/questions/230520/origin-of-a-rising-tide-lifts-all-boats

11 Kennedy, John F. *John F. Kennedy on the Economy & Taxes*. Boston, MA. The John F. Kennedy Presidential Library & Museum. https://www.jfklibrary.org/JFK/JFK-in-History/JFK-on-the-Economy-and-Taxes.aspx.

12 Economic Recovery Tax Act of 1981. https://www.congress.gov/bill/97th-congress/house-bill/4242

13 Kessler, Andy. *To Serve the Public, Seek Profits*. Wall Street Journal. https://www.andykessler.com/andy_kessler/2020/10/wsj-profits-not-greedy.html. October 12, 2020.

14 Johnson, Lyndon B. Commencement speech, University of Michigan. May 22, 1964.

15 Reagan, Ronald. Inaugural speech, January 20, 1981. https://www.reaganfoundation.org/ronald-reagan/reagan-quotes-speeches/inaugural-address-2/

Chapter 7

1   Sir Thomas More's *Utopia*. https://www.bl.uk/learning/timeline/item126618.html

2   https://languages.oup.com/dictionaries/

3   https://www.bl.uk/learning/timeline/item126618.html

4   Hazlitt, Henry. *Why Some are Poorer*. January 1, 1972. https://fee.org/articles/why-some-are-poorer/

5   Harrison, Maureen and Gilbert, Steve. *Abraham Lincoln: In His Own Words*. Excellent Books and Barnes & Noble, 1996.

6   Thatcher, Margaret. Speech to the Conservative Central Council, The Historic Choice, March 20, 1976. https://www.margaretthatcher.org/document/102990

7   Keys, Alan L. Quoted October 1992. Compiled by Bill Adler. *The Quotable Conservative: The Wit, Wisdom, and Insight of Freedom's Most Passionate Advocates*. Carol Publishing Group. 1996.

8   Sowell, Thomas. *Survival of the Left*, September 8, 1997, Forbes Magazine.

Chapter 8

1   https://www.bea.gov

2   https://www.federalregister.gov/documents/2020/03/18/2020-05794/declaring-a-national-emergency-concerning-the-novel-coronavirus-disease-covid-19-outbreak

3   https://www.bea.gov

4   https://www.bea.gov

5   https://www.fdrlibrary.org/great-depression-facts

6   About the CARES Act and the Consolidated Appropriations Act. U.S. Department of the Treasury. https://home.treasury.gov/policy-issues/coronavirus/about-the-cares-act

7   Accounting for Federal COVID Expenditures in the National Health Expenditure Accounts. https://www.cms.gov/files/document/accounting-federal-covid-expenditures-national-health-expenditure-accounts.pdf

8   Lebrecque, Leon. *The Cares Act Has Passed, Here are the Highlights*. March 29, 2020. https://www.forbes.com/sites/leonlabrecque/2020/03/29/the-cares-act-has-passed-here-are-the-highlights/?sh=1519dbb068cd

9   https://www.bea.gov

10   Ibid.

11   Hansen, Sarah and Ponciano, Jonathan. Finally: Trump Signs $900 Billion Relief Bill Clearing Way for $600 Stimulus Checks and Averting Shutdown.

December 27, 2020. https://www.forbes.com/sites/sarahhansen/2020/12/27/trump-signs-stimulus-package-600-checks-covid-relief/?sh=4a0891c245fc

12 Brewster, Jack. *Congress Passes $900 Billion Stimulus Bill Including $600 Checks and More Unemployment – But Leaves Out Student Loan Relief.* December 21, 2020. https://www.forbes.com/sites/jackbrewster/2020/12/21/congress-passes-900-billion-stimulus-bill-including-600-checks-and-more-unemployment---but-leaves-out-student-loan-relief/?sh=5d3d8fd540f5

13 American Rescue Plan Act of 2021. https://www.congress.gov/bill/117th-congress/house-bill/1319

14 https://www.bea.gov

15 https://cdc.gov

16 Kuhfeld, M., Soland, J., Lewis, K., Morton, E., *The Pandemic has had Devastating Impacts on Learning. What Will it Take to Help Students Catch Up?* March 3, 2022. Brookings Institution.

17 Rankin, David F., Interview, Talk Business and Politics, December 2020. www.davidfrankin.com

18 Musk, Elon. Interview, 2020.

Chapter 9

1 www.briannica.com

2 Quick Facts California. The U.S. Census Bureau. www.census.gov

3 Ibid.

4 https://taxfoundation.org/state-income-tax-rates

5 https://taxfoundation.org/2022-state-business-tax-climate-index/

6 Assembly Bill 1346 (Berman, Marc). https://ww2.arb.ca.gov/2021-assembly-bill-1346-berman-marc-small-road-engines-chaptered

7 Office of Labor Standards, Seattle, Washington.

8 California Legislation Information: AB-5 Worker Status: Employees and Independent Contractors. https://leginfo.legislature.ca.gov/faces/billNavClient.xhtml?bill_id=201920200AB5

Chapter 10

1 Friedman, Milton. *Money Mischief: Episodes in Monetary History.* (First) Harcourt Brace Jovanovich. 1992.

2 Hyperinflation. https://www.johndclare.net/Weimar_hyperinflation.htm

3   Backhouse, Fid. Hyperinflation in the Weimar Republic. German History. *Encyclopedia Britannica,* May 6, 2022. https://www.britannica.com/event/hyperinflation-in-the-weimar-republic.

4   www.statistica.com

5   Globerman, Steven. May 18, 2021. The Fraser Institute. https://www.fraserinstitute.org/studies/primer-on-modern-monetary-theory

6   Congressional Budget Office. The Federal Budget in Fiscal Year 2020: An Infographic. April 30, 2021. https://www.cbo.gov/publication/57170.

7   www.irs.gov

8   U.S. Bureau of Labor Statistics. *Consumer Prices up 9.1% Over the Year Ended June 2022, Largest Increase in 40 Years.* July 18, 2022. www.bls.gov

Chapter 11

1   Bureau of Economic Analysis. www.bea.gov

2   Congressional Budget Office. The 2020 Long-Term Budget Outlook. September 21, 2020. https://www.cbo.gov/publication/56516

3   O'Neill, Aaron. June 22, 2022. National Debt of Japan from 2017 to 2027. www.statista.com/

4   Federal Reserve Bank of St. Louis, www.fred.stlouis.fed.org/release/tables?rid=53&eid=12998#snid=12999

5   www.fred.stlouisfed.org/series/FYFSD

6   Harrison, M., and Gilbert, S. (1993), *Thomas Jefferson: In His Own Words.* Excellent Books in arrangement with Barnes & Noble, Inc., New York

Chapter 12

1   https://taxsummaries.pwc.com/france/individual/taxes-on-personal-income

2   Ang, Carmen. Tax-to-GDP Ratio: Comparing Tax Systems Around the World. July 28, 2021. Visual Capitalist. https://www.visualcapitalist.com/comparing-tax-systems-around-the-world/

3   https://www.oecd.org/tax/revenue-statistics-united-states.pdf

4   Reinsch, William A. Center for Strategic and International Studies. Don't Tax Me, Don't Tax Thee, Tax the Fellow Behind the Tree. https://www.csis.org/analysis/dont-tax-me-dont-tax-thee-tax-fellow-behind-tree

5   Library of Congress, *This Month in Business History: Income Tax Day.* https://guides.loc.gov/this-month-in-business-history/april/tax-day

6   Historical U.S. Federal Individual Income Tax Rates and Brackets, 1862-2021. Tax Foundation, August 24,2021. https://taxfoundation.org/historical-income-tax-rates-brackets/

7   Milton Friedman, Interview. https://www.youtube.com/watch?v=4gZ8pJZr8_g

Chapter 13

1   Federal Reserve History. The Banking Act of 1933 (Glass-Steagall). June 16, 1933. https://www.federalreservehistory.org/essays/glass-steagall-act

2   Federal Reserve History. The Banking Act of 1935. August 23, 1935. https://www.federalreservehistory.org/essays/banking-act-of-1935

3   New Deal. Encyclopedia Britannica. https://www.britannica.com/event/New-Deal

4   Ibid.

Chapter 14

1   Friedman, Milton (2002). *Capitalism and Freedom*. Fortieth anniversary. Originally published by the University of Chicago Press. 1962.

2   Forbes, Jr., Malcom. May 1993. Compiled by Bill Adler. *The Quotable Conservative: The Wit, Wisdom, and Insight of Freedom's Most Passionate Advocates*. Carol Publishing Group. 1996.

3   https://www.merriam-webster.com/dictionary/capitalism#:~:text=Definition%20of%20capitalism,competition%20in%20a%20free%20market

4   Zhao, Limount. Interview. September 3, 2021. https://www.youtube.com/watch?v=3n3tpAy-SCk

5   Schumpeter, Joseph (1943). *Socialism, Capitalism, and Democracy*.

6   Rice, Condoleezza. *Democracy: Stories from the Long Road to Freedom*. Twelve: Hachette Book Group. New York, NY, 2017.

7   Reagan, Ronald. April 19, 1986. https://www.reaganlibrary.gov/archives/speech/radio-address-nation-oil-prices

8   Friedman, Milton. *Capitalism and Freedom*.

9   Index of Economic Freedom, https://www.heritage.org/index/

10 10 Gramm, Phil. Quoted 1989. Compiled by Bill Adler. *The Quotable Conservative: The Wit, Wisdom, and Insight of Freedom's Most Passionate Advocates*. Carol Publishing Group. 1996.

11 Rier, Sharon. Half a Century Later, Economist's 'Creative Destruction' is apt for the Internet Age: Schumpeter: The Prophet of Bust and Boom. *New York Times*, June 10, 2000.

Chapter 15

1   Schumpeter, Joseph (1943). *Socialism, Capitalism, and Democracy.*
2   U.S. Customs and Border Protection. Southwest Land Border Encounters. https://www.cbp.gov/newsroom/stats/southwest-land-border-encounters
3   Forbes World Billionaire List. www.forbes.com
4   *The Law.* The Foundation for Economic Education, Inc. 17th printing. (p.67). 1993.
5   Solomon. Ecclesiastes 1:9. https://www.biblegateway.com/passage/?search=Ecclesiastes%201%3A9&version=NIV
6   Chernow, R. (2016). Alexander Hamilton. Head of Zeus, Ltd.
7   Eisenhower, Dwight, D. June 8, 1964. Compiled by Bill Adler. *The Quotable Conservative: The Wit, Wisdom, and Insight of Freedom's Most Passionate Advocates.* Carol Publishing Group. 1996.
8   Locke, John. The Second Treatise of Government. Originally published 1690. New York, NY: Barnes & Noble, Inc. 2004.
9   Pennsylvania Assembly: Reply to the Governor, November 11, 1755. https://founders.archives.gov/documents/Franklin/01-06-02-0107#:~:text=Those%20who%20would%20give%20up,deserve%20neither%20Liberty%20nor%20Safety.
10 The Tax Foundation. www.taxfoundation.org
11 Organization for Economic Cooperation and Development, www.oecd.org
12 The Tax Foundation. www.taxfoundation.org
13 Bureau of Labor Statistics, Inflation Calculator.
14 Durante, Alex. October 2022. The Tax Foundation. 2023 Tax Brackets https://taxfoundation.org/publications/federal-tax-rates-and-tax-brackets/
15 MacArthur, Douglas. Speech, May 3, 1948. Compiled by Bill Adler. The Quotable Conservative: *The Wit, Wisdom, and Insight of Freedom's Most Passionate Advocates.* Carol Publishing Group. 1996.
16 www.newsgallup.com
17 Keynes, John Maynard (1936). *The General Theory of Employment, Interest, and Money.*
18 Simpson, Alan K. The New York Times, September 26, 1982. Compiled by Bill Adler. *The Quotable Conservative: The Wit, Wisdom, and Insight of Freedom's Most Passionate Advocates.* Carol Publishing Group. 1996.